The Angels perverted the Creat...
but it was in Babylon th...
That very relig... ...n today as...

# MYSTERY BABYLON
## The Religion of The Beast

Revelation 17:5
The name written on her forehead was
a mystery: Babylon the great
the mother of prostitutes and of
the abominations of the earth.

by Rav Sha'ul

# Mystery Babylon

### *The Religion of The Beast*

# Book Two in
# The Original Revelation Series

## by
# Rav Sha'ul

I would like to thank my wife Stephanie you are the love of my life and my gift from Yahuah. I dedicate this book to my children Stephanie Yates, Ashley Black, Alexis Fox, and Dane Sides, may you all walk the path of righteousness and overcome the lie presented in this book.

Special Thanks to all those that contributed to this book and for your labour of love
And Special Thanks to Our Creator, Yahuah, For Everything!
"WE PROFESS YAHUSHA AS OUR MESSIAH

As I was writing this book, today is May 8, 2012. I was using Google to research the ancient pagan religions and this is the Google banner, it is of a researcher looking over ancient artifacts. Is this a Coincidence? I don't believe in coincidences.

In this image above notice the two smallest articles? They are the two tablets of Yahuah's Law on the very far left all alone **outside** of the shaded box of human tradition overshadowed by pagan relics!

This picture clearly says exactly what I am explaining in this book series. Yahuah does truly work in mysterious ways. It would seem the research above is going to have to look through and beyond all the pagan relics and idols to find The Truth.

# Table of Contents

# Preface

In the first book of the Original Revelation series: "Creation Cries Out!"- we took a journey back to the origin of mankind to determine where sun worship originated. We discovered that it was Yahuah, The Creator, who authored the message found within the heavens. That message is foretold in The Zodiac as it was Yahuah Who named every star, organized them into constellations, and gave those constellations their name and meaning.

In that first book, I also demonstrated the Bible clearly indicates that Yahuah was the Author of The Zodiac and further showed how it was the fallen angles and their offspring (The Nephilim) that corrupted The Zodiac and the message it proclaimed. The corrupted version of The Zodiac message resulted in the worship of the creation over The Creator. Mankind began worshipping incarnate man-gods, the Sun, Moon, Constellations, and the anthropomorphic animal signs of The Zodiac. We learned from the Book of Enoch how fallen angels gave advanced knowledge to mankind and taught astrology, witchcraft, and sorcery. If you haven't read the first book, *Creation Cries Out!*, I strongly suggest you do because each book of *The Original Revelation Series* builds on the one before.

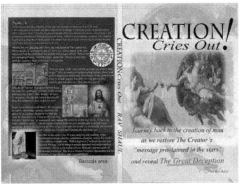

Available on TheBookPatch.com

In the second book of the ***Original Revelation Series***: **Mystery Babylon** – *The Religion of the Beast,* we are going to define how sun worship (that originated with the Sumerian Culture some 5,000 years ago) was organized later into a World Religion in Babylon. This religion evolved complete with a well defined Godhead, a day of worship, holy days, a Christ, and sacrifices. This religion, The Mystery Religion of Babylon, is the false religion identified in Scripture.

It was this first world religion that was scattered among all nations and cultures at The Tower of Babel when Yahuah confused the languages. We can trace through time and cultures the progression of this religion as humanity flourished on Earth to the present day. Before we can identify what religion today is The Mystery Religion of Babylon, we must first clearly define this world religion as it existed in ancient Babylon. Only then can we compare the religions of today to find an exact match. Then we must compare this false religion to the "Faith" described in The Bible and identify The Truth. That is the purpose of my book series The Original Revelation. Throughout this book series, we carefully examine the evolution of history as man has built upon the corrupted version of the message written in the stars.

As I explained in the first book, ***Creation Cries Out!,*** mankind was taught a perverted version of the message found in The Zodiac and began to personify that message into "myths" around The Grand Man creating for themselves incarnate man-gods called Christs. Man then began making idols that represented the signs of The Zodiac to worship them. It was in Babylon that the personification of the "strong man" found in The Zodiac represented by the Sun, was personified as a real living man… Nimrod. An entire false religion was built around the personification of The Sun as Nimrod who became known as Ba'al the Sungod. The battle began between these false messiahs and the True prophesied Messiah to come. A battle that is prevalent and takes center stage throughout the Bible, and that battle continues today.

Babylon is the first great city after Adam was created. Its founder, Nimrod, was the great grandson of Noah and his name is found in the genealogies in the Book of Genesis and the Book of Chronicles. The life of Nimrod is covered in detail in the book of Jasher. Nimrod is described as a very powerful man and a great hunter. Nimrod founded several cities in ancient Mesopotamia and was King over all the sons of Noah. Babylon became a center for ancient thought and commerce and it is from Babylon that the worship of the orbiting planets in our solar system became worshipped as gods.

The Sun was worshipped as the highest god of all and Sun worship became what we know today as *The Mystery Religion of Babylon*. It is this worship of the Sun and planets that has been the center of paganism since the founding of Babylon and the "reason" behind the construction of the "Tower of Babel" ... to reach the stars/gods and prevent another "great flood" and avenge humanity against Yahuah, Who had previously destroyed their forefathers in the days of Noah. It was in Babylon that the first concept of "One World Government" originated. The Tower of Babel was to be the greatest pagan Temple to the Sungod ever created.

Pieter Bruegel's *The Tower of Babel* depicts
a traditional Nimrod inspecting stonemasons.

In the book of Jasher, Nimrod is described in the following manner
"And all the Earth was of one tongue and words of union, but
Nimrod did not go in the ways of Yahuah, and he was the most
wicked of all the men that were before Yahuah, from the days of
the flood until those days." Judaic interpreters as early as Philo and
Yochanan ben Zakai (1st century AD) interpreted "a mighty hunter
*before* Yahuah" (Heb. : לפני יהוה, lit. "*in the face of Yahuah*") as
signifying "*in opposition to* Yahuah"; a similar interpretation is
found in Pseudo-Philo, as well as later in Symmachus. Some
rabbinic commentators have also connected the name *Nimrod* with
a Hebrew word meaning 'rebel'.   The great Jewish Historian
Josephus writes:

> *"Now it was Nimrod who excited them to such an affront
> and contempt of God. He was the grandson of Ham, the son
> of Noah, a bold man, and of great strength of hand. He
> persuaded them not to ascribe it to God, as if it were
> through his means they were happy, but to believe that it
> was their own courage which procured that happiness. He
> also gradually changed the government into tyranny,
> seeing no other way of turning men from the fear of God,
> but to bring them into a constant dependence on his power.
> He also said he would be revenged on God, if he should
> have a mind to drown the world again; for that he would
> build a tower to high for the waters to reach. And that he
> would avenge himself on God for destroying their
> forefathers.*

> *Now the multitude were very ready to follow the
> determination of Nimrod, and to esteem it a piece of
> cowardice to submit to God; and they built a tower, neither
> sparing any pains, nor being in any degree negligent about
> the work: and, by reason of the multitude of hands
> employed in it, it grew very high, sooner than anyone could
> expect; but the thickness of it was so great, and it was so*

11

*strongly built, that thereby its great height seemed, upon the view, to be less than it really was. It was built of burnt brick, cemented together with mortar, made of bitumen, that it might not be liable to admit water.*

*When God saw that they acted so madly, he did not resolve to destroy them utterly, since they were not grown wiser by the destruction of the former sinners; but he caused a tumult among them, by producing in them diverse languages, and causing that, through the multitude of those languages, they should not be able to understand one another.*

*The place wherein they built the tower is now called Babylon, because of the confusion of that language which they readily understood before; for the Hebrews mean by the word Babel, confusion...*

Today, it is this very religious system and "world government system" that began with Nimrod, that is behind Freemasonry and the Illuminati. Nimrod figures in some very early versions of the history of Freemasonry, where he was said to have been one of the fraternity's founders.

**According to the Encyclopedia of Freemasonry:** *The legend of the Craft in the Old Constitutions* refers to Nimrod as one of the founders of Masonry. Thus in the York MS., No. 1, we read:

> *"At ye making of ye toure of Babell there was a Masonrie first much esteemed of, and the King of Babylon called Nimrod was a Mason himself and loved well Masons."*

In this chapter, I am going to explain what that "Mystery" religion believed. I will explain how it was formulated, and how it progressed over time through many cultures as Nimrod "died" and was believed to become The Sun. I will explain how Nimrod was then later worshipped as the reincarnated Tammuz who was believed to be the son of the sungod Ba'al in the flesh. Tammuz was the first of the false god-men incarnations of "god". Both Nimrod and Tammuz were the literal sons of Semaramis creating the first "Trinity Godhead". The son was the incarnation of the father, the father became the son, both were the wife and son of the mother. Every aspect of that same religion and government system survives today as I will explain.

Every ritual remains the same, the name of the god remains a later incarnation of Tammuz, and The LORD god Ba'al has replaced Yahuah.

### 1 Kings 18

[18] "I have not made trouble for Israel," Elijah replied. "But you and your father's family have. **You have abandoned Yahuah's Commands and have followed Baal** (*The Lord*).

### Jeremiah 23

[25] "I have heard what the prophets say who prophesy lies in My Name… [26] How long will this continue in the hearts of these lying prophets, who prophesy the delusions of their own minds? [27] They think the dreams they tell one another will make My people forget My Name, **just as their ancestors forgot My Name through Baal (*The Lord*) worship**.

Most people do not realize that when they address Yahuah as "The Lord" they are doing exactly as stated above and calling upon Baal:

http://en.wikipedia.org/wiki/Baal

> *Baal, also rendered Ba'al (Biblical Hebrew בַּעַל), is a Northwest Semitic title and honorific meaning "master" or "lord" that is used for various gods who were patrons of cities in the Levant and Asia Minor, cognate to Akkadian Bēlu. A Baalist or Baalite means a worshipper of Baal i.e.*

*The Lord. "Ba'al" or "The Lord" can refer to any god and even to human officials.*

*In some texts it is used for Hadad, a god of the rain, thunder, fertility and agriculture, and the lord of heaven. Since only priests were allowed to utter His Divine name, Hadad, Ba'al was commonly used. Nevertheless, few if any Biblical uses of "Ba'al" refer to Hadad, the lord over the assembly of gods on the holy mount of heaven; most refer to a variety of local spirit-deities worshipped as cult images, each called ba'al and regarded in the Hebrew Bible in that context as a "false god".*

*Etymology - Ba'al (bet-ayin-lamedh) is a Semitic word signifying "The Lord, master, owner (male), keeper, husband"*

Now let us fully define the religion created in Babylon; the rituals, the gods, and the day of worship. This is of extreme importance as Peter called Rome Babylon; and Yahusha Commanded we come out of her, (Mystery Babylon the Great Whore) for she will deceived the entire planet by the time Yahusha returns. As we define this abomination, which is sun worship passed down from Babylon to Rome, I am sure the false religion today will begin to show its true colors.

# Chapter 1

## *How the Mystery Religion was formulated*

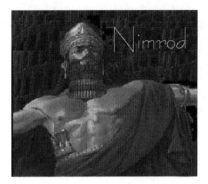

# The Legacy of Nimrod – The Sun God Ba'al

Nimrod worshipped the pagan sungod named Moloch. The title "Great Hunter before (in the face of) Yahuah" was ascribed to him because he literally hunted human beings to murder as sacrifices to his pagan god. In the book of Jasher (the book of Jasher is mentioned in the Bible in Joshua 10:13 and 2 Samuel 1:18 and was conveniently left out by The Catholic Church for obvious reasons), we learn that Nimrod received instruction from the priests of Moloch to marry his mother in an act of incest in order to acquire "the third eye" or the "all seeing eye". The exact same knowledge sought by those today who call themselves the "illuminati" or "illuminated ones" who consider Nimrod the first High Mason. This form of "dark knowledge" is a counterfeit of The Spirit of Yahuah with a Promise to "see" into the spiritual realm. The universal sign of this "dark knowledge" is the "Eye of Ra" floating above the unfinished tower of Babel making the shape of an Egyptian Pyramid.

All-seeing-eye of Lucifer (Light Bearer)

Yes, this is "the god" of our so-called Christian Nation found on the back of the dollar bill. Once I explain the origins of Christianity it will become obvious in which "God we trust" and it is not and has never been Yahuah. Today, the USA is by far the greatest abomination the Earth has ever seen. Waging unjust "crusades" across the globe and dumping filth into the minds of humanity through its entertainment system. This country is built upon everything that is unholy to Yahuah. It's leaders participating in Moloch worship and human sacrifice at Bohemian Grove, CA annually. Google it!

The legacy of Nimrod is human sacrifice to Moloch which was the image of a "bull" that the Israelites constructed at the foot of Mt. Sinai (the reason for Yahuah's furry).

This ritual sacrifice continues today as our highest level world leaders, business leaders, and entertainment moguls participate each year in what is called "The Cremation of Care". In this ritual they sacrifice a human on the altar of Moloch. In doing so, these world leaders sacrifice their compassion/conscience and "care" for humanity as they carry out the Illuminati agenda of world depopulation through wars, starvation, weather control, and more.

The list of "known" participants in this abomination reads like a "who's who" of famous world leaders throughout history.

All coming to the US (the spiritual seat of Babylon) to sacrifice their conscience on the altar of Moloch! I digress; that is another book all together, it is outside the scope of this book. Let's get back to the topic at hand.

# The abomination of the Trinity is born in Babylon

Nimrod the King, took a wife. The wife Nimrod chose was his mother. So the "son" became both the husband and son of the mother. In effect this marriage created a "trinity" union in as much as the "husband" was the same person as the "son" united as "one" with the wife/mother through marriage. So Nimrod married his mother, Semaramis, and she became the Queen of Babylon also known as The Queen of Heaven (a title for the Virgin Mary). It was Semaramis from which the "religion" surrounding Nimrod and the planets (astrology) evolved. Nimrod the mighty and ruthless murderer was killed for his crimes against humanity. His body cut into pieces and distributed all over his kingdom by his enemies.

# The rise of the Queen of Heaven - Semaramis

After Nimrod's death, Semaramis his mother/wife/queen had to maintain her grip and power over the people. In order to solidify her power she invented a religion for the people that would keep Nimrod's control over them even after his death. She then gave birth to a son named *Tammuz* whom she claimed was the reincarnation of Nimrod or the son of the sungod, the incarnation of God, God in the flesh. So Tammuz was "Nimrod in the flesh" and "one" with his father who was "one" with his wife/mother through marriage. Semaramis was the mother of God… the Trinity is born.

The Babylonian Empire was the first attempt at a "One World Government" or "New World Order". This human attempt at global governance through the use of "dark knowledge", astrology, and pagan god worship was an abomination to Yahuah. The Tower of Babel was a tower built not to literally "reach up to Yahuah", but rather as a massive structure from which to consult the stars through the use of astrology and communicate with "The Sun" The LORD god Baal. Yahuah intervened and confused the speech of the people of Earth and scattered them abroad. With the migration of the people coming out of Babylon, the sun-worshipping religion of Babylon was scattered throughout the Earth, the names changed but the religion remained the same to the smallest detail.

Since the languages now were "confused" the names of Nimrod, Semaramis, and Tammuz were changed and continued to change over time based on culture and language. Although the names changed, the religion remained exactly the same. Semaramis, however, became known as "The Queen of Heaven" among all cultures and worshipped as the primary head of this false religion.

The Pope of Rome has even dedicated the 7<sup>th</sup> Millennium (which is prophetically The Sabbath Millennium when Yahusha reigns on Earth) to… The Queen of Heaven:

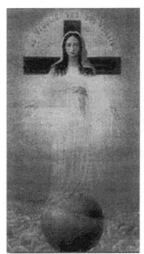

*Mary (Isis/Ishtar/Semaramis) standing in mediation between mankind and Yahusha the Messiah... the Co-Redemptix idolatry of Catholicism.*
http://www.nytimes.com/1987/01/02/world/pope-proclaims-a-year-dedicated-to-virgin-

mary.html

Even the children of Israel fell into the worship of Semaramis, The Queen of Heaven, and Yahuah sent them the Prophet Jeremiah with the following warning:

## Jeremiah 44:17-18

"But we will certainly do whatsoever thing goes forth out of our own mouth, to burn incense unto the QUEEN OF HEAVEN, and to pour out drink offerings unto her, as we have done, we, and our fathers, our kings, and our princes, in the cities of Judah, and in the streets of Jerusalem: for then had we plenty of victuals, and were well, and saw no evil. But since we left off to burn incense to the QUEEN OF HEAVEN, and to pour out drink offerings unto her, we have wanted all things, and have been consumed by the sword and by the famine."

The statue to the left was originally a statue of *Semaramis holding Tammuz* in Babylon then renamed *Isis holding Horus* in Egypt. Later, the Roman idol became the *Madonna/Child*. Finally, the religion of Christianity renamed this idol *Mary/Jesus*.

This statue was literally renamed by the Roman Emperor Constantine to "Mary and Baby Jesus" in the 3rd Century as the names continued to evolve and change while the religion remained the same. We will discuss these name changes later in this book series and prove that Jesus H. Christ was created in the image of 3 pagan incarnated god-men, the Druid god Hesus, the Egyptian god Horus, and the Eastern god Krishna, each one just Tammuz in another cutler. The name given to the new god of Christianity by Constantine of "Hesus Horus Krishna" evolved over the last 1,500 years. The I in the Greek *Iesus* grew a tail and became a J, *Horus*

21

was abbreviated to H., and **Krishna** went from Sanskrit to English as Christ… "Jesus H. Christ". The true Messiah's name in Hebrew was Yahusha. The English translation is Joshua. We will cover more of this abomination in my next book, **Christianity: *The Great Deception***. Available on www.sabbathcovenant.com.

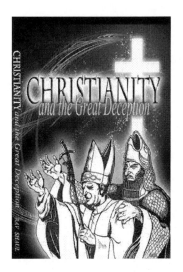

Together, Semaramis and Nimrod (her son/husband) started this occult religion of sacrificing babies to Moloch, aka Satan or the false pagan sun-god. Nimrod means "tyrant," as he led the Babylonians to pay tribute to the skies (the sun, moon, stars, and planets) with the sacrifices of their children. The Tower of Babel, which was built for this purpose among others, was echoed in other cultures such as the Egyptians, Aztecs, Mayans, and Incas in the form of Pyramid structures all aligned with the Sun and all built for the same purposes as The Tower of Babel. The same image of the Pyramid with the detached all Seeing Eye adorns our dollar bill clearly identifying the "god in whom we trust". They are pagan Temples dedicated to sun worship that evolved from Babylon.

The picture above is a depiction of children being sacrificed to the two horned god Moloch (Satan), even today this practice is "simulated" by our world leaders at Bohemian Grove in California each year as I mentioned.

# The Obelisk

Obelisks were constructed as part of this "religion" as phallic or male fertility symbols interpreted as sun rays.

These exact same pagan structures are echoed throughout our "Christian" nations. A massive obelisk sits in the very center of St. Peter's Square of The Vatican (birthplace and capital city of Christianity) in Rome surrounded by Occult symbols and figures and idols of pagan gods.

Notice above the obelisk is in the center of The Zodiac. The Vatican is THE pagan Temple of sun worship. And we have an obelisk constructed in the heart of our own "Christian" nation we call The Washington Monument. This is a monument to the The Mystery Religion of Babylon.

These obelisks, to this day, grace the tops of Christian Churches, we just call them "steeples" adorned with the "Cross of Tammuz" (I will cover this too, in this book series) as we worship The Trinity on Sun-god-Day.

Christians are still 100% Catholic in doctrine they are just "**protest**ing Catholics" called "**Protest**ants".

This religion created in Babylon by Nimrod and Semaramis was making them rich as the people had to pay money to come into the temple to sacrifice their babies at the Winter Solstice i.e. Christmas (December 21st-25th) and also at "Easter (Ishtar) Sunrise Services," at the spring or Vernal Equinox (March 21st-25th).

Every year on March 25th & December 25th, there would be wild drunken parties and orgies where virgins were impregnated by pagan priests. Since there are 9 months to a pregnancy, and there are also 9 months between March 25th and December 25th, the pagan priests of Ba'al would impregnate these virgins on Easter Sunday in ritual dedicated to Ba'al to commemorate the impregnation of Semaramis with Tammuz. Then by December

25th when these infants were newly born, the priests of Ba'al would offer up these new born babies on the altar to "Moloch" (Nimrod). A few months later, on Ishtar Day which in English is Easter "Sun-day", they would offer up more infants to the goddess named "Easter" or "Ishtar" the fertility moon goddess Semaramis. They would then take the blood of these sacrificed infants and dip "eggs" in them (called **Ishtar Eggs**). Let's take a closer look at this religion as it is beginning to sound familiar.

# Religion of Semaramis
## *The Moon Goddess Ishtar*

As I was saying… Nimrod was killed by his enemies and his body parts distributed all over his kingdom. Semaramis attempted to gather the body parts of Nimrod. Semaramis accomplished retrieving all parts of his dismembered body except his "private parts". It was from the private parts of Nimrod that Semaramis created the fertility religion known as *The Mystery Religion of Babylon.* These private parts were commemorated by the construction of Obelisks which, as I mentioned, are one of the most prevalent of Christian symbols. Semaramis is described by ancient Greek historians this way:

> *Herodotus (about 484-420 B.C.) describes her as a queen who ruled the whole of Asia. Diodorus (first century A.D.) says she was the daughter of the Syrian goddess Derketo of Askalon and describes her celebrated construction of the splendid city of Babylon with its hanging gardens, which since modern times have been counted as one of the Seven Wonders of the Ancient World. He also portrays her as a man-eating queen and powerful warrior, who defeated the powerful army of the Medes. Athenagoras of Athens (second century A.D.), one of the Apologists, calls Semaramis, in his work Legatio pro Christianis, "an immoral and murderous woman."*

After the death of her son/husband King Nimrod, Semaramis began to formulate what we now know as *The Mystery Religion of Babylon* to secure her reign of power. In her new religion, she proclaimed that Nimrod had defeated death and elevated himself above all that is called "god" and literally became The Sun. This was easily accepted by mankind because The Zodiac message had already been corrupted by the fallen angels and man had been indoctrinated since the Sumerian Culture to worship the sun. I covered that in my last book, *Creation Cries Out!.*

26

Semaramis instituted a day of worship dedicated to the sun that even today, we call "Sun-day". Sunday is English for the Latin 'Dies Solis' which means "Day of the Invincible Sun". This pagan day of worship later replaced The Day of Rest, the 7th Day Sabbath by order of the sun worshipping Emperor Constantine (I will go into this in great detail later).

Semaramis, being the mother of Nimrod in addition to his queen, elevated herself up as "The Mother of God" and "Queen of Heaven" and called herself the goddess Ishtar. Semaramis later became pregnant, not wanting to destroy her "image" as the Queen/Mother of God, declaring Nimrod (the Sun God now called **_Ba'al_** later known as Zeus by the Greeks then The LORD in Christianity) had impregnated her through the "rays of the sun". She had given a "virgin birth" to her new son named Tammuz who she claimed was the "reincarnated Nimrod", the incarnation of God in the flesh, and The Son of "God". Tammuz became the second member of The Trinity. So Tammuz was believed to be the sungod Baal (Nimrod) in the flesh and at the same time The Son of God. The two, Semaramis and Tammuz, became worshipped as what we now know as "Madonna and Child" then later Mary/Jesus as all the idols were simply renamed by different cultures.

# Legend of Tammuz

Tammuz was a great hunter like his (supposed) father Nimrod. Tammuz was killed by a wild pig in a hunting accident. Semaramis then expanded on her new religion explaining that her "immortal god-son" who "died" was "resurrected" and became "one with his father", the Sungod Baal. The Trinity was further defined. Nimrod, Semaramis, and Tammuz became worshipped as the Divine Godhead, a triune god in opposition to Yahuah (the one and only true living God). This is the origin of the Christian Trinity. The "son" was the "father", the father the "son", and both "one" with the mother through marriage.

This is documented by many authoritative sources:

> ***The Religions of Ancient Greece and Babylonia***, by A. H. Sayce. pages 229-230, clearly tells us that the Greek philosophical ideas were developed in Alexandria, Egypt from the pagan mystery religions.

>> *Many of the theories of Egyptian religion, modified and transformed no doubt, have penetrated into the theology of Christian Europe, and form, as it were, part of the woof in the web of modern religious thought. Christian theology was largely organized and nurtured in the schools of Alexandria, and Alexandria was not only the meeting place of East and West, it was also the place where the decrepit theology of Egypt was revivified by contact with the speculative philosophy of Greece. Perhaps, however, the indebtedness of Christian theological theory to ancient Egyptian dogma is nowhere more striking than in the doctrine of the Trinity. The very terms used of it by Christian theologians meet us again in the inscriptions and papyri of Egypt. Originally the trinity was a triad **like those we find in Babylonian mythology**. The triad consisted of a divine father, wife, and son. The father became the son and the son the father through all time, and of both alike the mother was but another form.*

> ***The Outline of History***, by H. G. Wells. page 307, tells us:

>> The trinity consisted of the god Serapis (=Osiris+Apis), the goddess Isis (=Hathor, the cow-moon goddess), and the child-god Horus. In one way or another almost every other god was identified with one or the other of these three aspects of the one god, even the sun god Mithras of the Persians. And they were each other; they were three, but they were also one.

I will go into great detail on The Trinity in later chapters and in my next book, *'Christianity and The Great Deception'*.

Armed with her new religion, Semaramis continued on conquering and expanding her "world government system" and was a very powerful effective ruler over much of Assyria. In the interest of staying on point, I will not go into much more detail concerning the historical and legendary records of Nimrod and Semaramis. I suggest the reader conduct independent study if necessary. This chapter is only intended to <u>define the religion</u> created by Semaramis known as the Goddess Ishtar/Isis/Diana/Mary, among other names. That religion has come to be known as *The Mystery Religion of Babylon*. It must be fully defined so that we can identify how that religion evolved to this very day and has, as prophesied by Yahuah, deceived all humanity for 2000 years.

For more on the Mystery Religion of Babylon, please read:

http://doubleportioninheritance.blogspot.com/2012/02/queen-of-heaven-why-does-church.html

# Chapter 2

## *What is "The Mystery Religion of Babylon"?*

# What is The Mystery Religion of Babylon?

The religion created by Semaramis (Ishtar) flourished over time and began to take definition. Like the True Faith in Yahuah, this new counterfeit religion had <u>holy days</u>, <u>sacrifices</u>, <u>a day of worship</u>, etc. that identified this religion over time as it progressed from one culture to the next. Ultimately, to be re-established in Rome as the seat of this religion, as I pointed out in the first book *Creation Cries Out!*.

Nimrod became Baal the Sun God, Semaramis became Ishtar the fertility Goddess, and Tammuz was worshipped as the Son of God incarnate/God in the flesh to form *The Trinity*. <u>The Trinity is the defining pretense/doctrine of all pagan religions and all of them can be traced back to Baal, Ishtar, and Tammuz.</u>

It is not my intention in this book to contest the "Christian Trinity" but to simply show that the Trinitarian doctrine is the foundation of EVERY religion but one… The True Faith in Yahuah which declares the basic premise that Yahuah alone is God and there is no other (The Faith held by Adam, Abraham, Isaac, Jacob, Moses, David, Solomon, Sampson, The Messiah Yahusha, all his disciples, and every early convert of the early church until 300 AD).

The *Encyclopedia Britannica,* Micropedia Volume 11, page 928, gives us the following facts about the trinity.

> *TRINITY, in Christian doctrine, the unity of Father, Son, and Holy Spirit as three persons in one Godhead. <u>Neither the word Trinity nor the explicit doctrine appears in the New Testament</u>, nor did Jesus and his followers intend to contradict <u>**the Shema**</u> in the Old Testament: "Hear, O Israel: Yahuah our God is one God" (Deuteronomy 6:4).*

> *The doctrine of The Trinity developed gradually over several centuries and through many controversies.*

It took many centuries and many controversies to establish The Trinity as it is not a concept found in The Bible. In fact, the modern English Bible translations had to be edited and perverted in order to "imply" the doctrine of The Trinity as I will prove in this book series. For more information on how the Bible has been altered, read the book 'Misquoting Jesus'.

Over many centuries a very well defined religion evolved from the beginnings in Babylon. The names vary depending on the culture and language but the basic structure remained. All later mystery pagan religions share a defined structure:

- Godhead – in the form of a trinity or triune gods
- A day of worshipping The Sungod called Sunday
- A "symbol" of the "son" of God, the cross of Tammuz a cut-out of the center of The Zodiac.
- A resurrection day celebration, on "Ishtar Day" commemorated on the Vernal (Spring) Equinox. When winter turns to spring each year around the end of March. The eating of a pig on Ishtar Day as the sacrifice to Tammuz.
- A holiday celebration of the annual rebirth of the Sun God on the Winter Solstice. This celebration is held each year on the shortest day of the year when the "Sun" is reborn and the days begin to get longer around December 25th.
- The second member of The Trinity who was the "incarnation" of God.

It is these six main aspects of **The Mystery Religion of Babylon** that I would like to focus on for the purpose of this book series. These are the identifying beliefs and rituals of the religion of Babylon. I define and explain each of them briefly. I will reference these main aspect and define the "**The Mystery Religion of Babylon**".

# Chapter 3

## The Pagan "Trinity"

# The Pagan "Trinity" – Overview

The pagan god worshipped in *The Mystery Religion of Babylon* was a triune god made up of *the Father/the incarnate Son/ and Mother of God*.  The father was the son, the son the father, and both were one with the mother in marriage (Semaramis married both Nimrod and her son Tammuz).  We see this abomination as a constant theme among pagan religions. The Trinity is condemned in The Bible as Yahuah is not a triune god but the One and Only Living God.  It is the worship of this triune "Trinity" representation of gods that opposes the God in The Bible.  Yahuah declares "you shall have no other gods before Me" … "Before Me" is the English translation of the Hebrew words "in My Face".  So Yahuah actually said "you shall have no other gods in My Face!" The same expression used of Nimrod who was described as a "mighty hunter before Yahuah' or rather a "mighty hunter in the Face of Yahuah" implying rebellion against Yahuah.  So we are to "have no other gods in Yahuah's Face!"

**NOTE:**  The declaration that Yahuah is ONE (not a Trinity) is the central theme in the True Faith of every man of God in the Bible, including The Messiah.  This Knowledge of Yahuah being the One and Only Creator, is the "mark" on the forehead of the Elect called "The Shema".  It is this mark, the Shema, that marks the elect for Eternal life.  When Yahusha (the True Messiah) was asked the single greatest Commandment of Yahuah, he quoted The Shema (Shema means "hear" in Hebrew) from The Torah.

### Mark 12:29

"The most important one," answered Yahusha, "is this: 'Hear, O Israel, Yahuah our God, **Yahuah is One**.

Yahusha was quoting Deuteronomy 6:4 verbatim.  This passage of Deuteronomy is also defined as the "mark between our eyes and on our right hands".  The Shema is THE "mark of Yahuah" that sets us apart from this "false religion" whose mark is the Trinity made on the foreheads of newly baptized babies. This false mark of the Trinity is also made over the hearts of literally billions every day.

This "mark" of Yahuah on our foreheads and right hand (displayed by The Messiah and expressed as the single greatest command as we see below) is an outright denial of the pagan Trinity gods:

### Deuteronomy 6

4 Hear, O Israel: ***Yahuah our God, Yahuah is One***. 5 Love Yahuah your God with all your heart and with all your soul and with all your strength. 6 These Commandments that I give you today are to be on your hearts. 7 Impress them on your children. Talk about them when you sit at home and when you walk along the road, when you lie down and when you get up. 8 Tie them as symbols (*mark*) on your hands and bind them (*mark*) on your foreheads.

The true Messiah Yahusha demonstrated this singular Knowledge of Yahuah is the foundation of Eternal life. For He is the Giver of life and to receive that life you must be in covenant with Yahuah through the Yahushaic Covenant:

### John 17:3

[3] **And this is Eternal life**, that they may know You (*Yahuah*), **the Only True God**, and (*then there is*) Yahusha (*the*) Messiah whom You (*Yahuah*) have sent (*as the Passover, not Easter sacrifice for sin*).

We also see this same triune god is a consistent theme in every pagan religion which evolved from *The Mystery Religion of Babylon*. This religion of Satan cleverly opposes the Mark of Yahuah in the mind ('mark on the forehead' is a metaphor for Knowledge) with what is called The Mark of the Beast defined later in this book series. For a very detailed look at the Beast and His Mark, please read my book, The Antichrist Revealed! available on my website www.sabbathcovenant.com. This book is a MUST READ for every human on this planet! In this book, I clearly identify the Antichrist or 'false messiah', his mark, the Abomination of Desolation, the Transgression of Desolation, and much more.

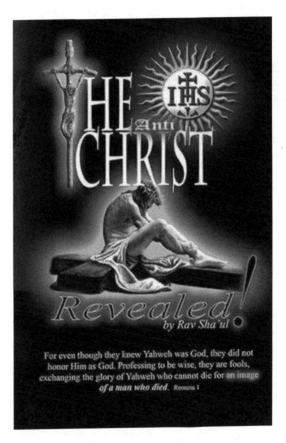

Let us take a look at The Trinity as it evolved over time throughout almost every culture. Before we begin, let us define the concept of a triune god.

# The History of the Pagan Trinity

Source: http://en.wikipedia.org/wiki/Triple_deity

**TRIPLE DEITY**

*A **triple deity** (sometimes referred to as threefold, Trinity, tripled, triplicate, tripartite, triune or triadic) is a deity associated with the number three. Such deities are common throughout world mythology; **the number three has a long history of mythical associations**. C. G. Jung considered the arrangement of deities into triplets an archetype (or mark) in the history of religion. The deities and legendary creatures of this nature typically fit into one of the following general categories:*

- *triadic* ("forming a group of three"): a triad, three entities inter-related in some way (life, death, rebirth, for example, or triplet children of a deity) and always or usually associated with one another or appearing together;

- *triune* ("three-in-one, one-in-three"): a Trinity being with three aspects or manifestations;

- *tripartite* ("of triple parts"): a being with three body parts where there would normally be one (three heads, three pairs of arms, and so on); or

- *triplicate-associated* ("relating to three corresponding instances"): a being in association with a trio of things of the same nature which are symbolic or through which power is wielded (three magic birds, etc.)

Now let us take a journey throughout history as The Trinity evolved as *THE 'god'* of almost every pagan religion in opposition to Yahuah, the ONLY TRUE GOD. We see The Messiah Yahusha speaking to his Heavenly Father, Yahuah, in John 17:3. He declares this simple truth and that truth is where Salvation is found:

## John 17:3

3 Now this is Eternal life: that they know You (*Yahuah*), **the Only True God**, and (*Your*) Messiah Yahusha, whom You have sent.

Again, when asked the single greatest Commandment in the entire Bible, Yahusha clearly contradicted the pagan Trinity. In Mark 12:28-34, the Messiah correctly answered the teachers of The Law with what is known as the Shema. This mark is the seal of Yahuah on your forehead... Yahusha quoted directly from Deuteronomy 12:

## Mark 12:28-34

28 One of the teachers of The Law came and heard them debating. Noticing that Yahusha had given them a good answer, he asked him, "Of all the Commandments, which is the most important?"

29 "The most important one," answered Yahusha, "is this: 'Hear, O Israel: Yahuah our God, Yahuah is (*The*) One (*and Only God*). 30 Love Yahuah your God with all your heart and with all your soul and with all your mind and with all your strength.'

So much for "the Trinity"... that is how pagans worship their gods, not how the men in the Bible, including The Messiah worshipped

Yahuah. Yahuah forbids us from "saying we are Worshipping Him" in the way pagans worship their gods:

**Deuteronomy 12:31**

You must not Worship Yahuah your God in their way, because in worshipping their gods, they do all kinds of detestable things Yahuah hates. They even burn their sons and daughters in the fire as sacrifices to their gods (Moloch worship).

No wonder Christianity abolished The Torah. It stands as Witness against every ritual they practice. Let's take a look at every pagan religion and their "Trinity' gods.

# ➢ The Egyptian Trinity

**NOTE: I.H.S. is the monogram of Jesus H. Christ or "Isis/Horus/Seb". The Egyptian Trinity of Isis, Horus, Seb (Egyptian names for Baal, Ishtar, Tammuz). The Outline of History, by H. G. Wells. page 307 tell us:**

"The Trinity consisted of the god Serapis (=Osiris+Apis), the goddess Isis/Ishtar (= Hathor, the cow-moon goddess), and the child-god Horus (the Egyptian Tammuz). In one way or another almost every other god was identified with one or the other of these three aspects of the one god, even the sun god Mithras of the Persians (*whom Constantine worshipped*). **The origin beginning with Baal, Ishtar, Tammuz of the ancient Babylonian Religion.** Many of the theories of Egyptian religion have penetrated into the theology of Christian Europe, and form, as it were, part of the woof in the web of modern religious thought. Christian theology was largely organized and nurtured in the schools of Alexandria, and Alexandria was not only the meeting place of East and West, it was also the place where the decrepit theology of Egypt was revivified by contact with the speculative philosophy of Greece. Perhaps, however, **the indebtedness of Christian theological theory to ancient Egyptian dogma is nowhere more striking than in the doctrine of the Trinity**. The very terms used of it by Christian theologians meet us again in the inscriptions and papyri of Egypt. **Originally the Trinity was a triad like those we find in Babylonian mythology**. The triad consisted of a divine father, wife, and son. **This triune god was later formulated into Christianity as the Christian Trinity of father, son, holy ghost**." End quote.

# ➤ The Hecate Trinity

**The Hecate Trinity (and the Statue of Liberty) …**

The Statue of Liberty, the Eye of Horus on the dollar bill, and the Obelisk (we call The Washington Monument) all identify our great country and the religion it is founded upon as modern day Babylon.

The Hecate Trinity was also associated with Diana (another cultural name of Ishtar). A triplefold Diana was venerated from the late sixth century BCE as Diana Nemorensis. "The Latin Diana was conceived as a threefold unity of the divine huntress, the Moon goddess, and the goddess of the nether world, Hekate," Albert Alföldi interpreted the late Republican numismatic image, noting that Diana *montium custos nemoremque virgo* ("keeper of the mountains and virgin of Nemi") is addressed by Horace as *diva triformis* ("three-form goddess"). Diana is commonly addressed as Trivia by Virgil and Catullus.

As a virgin goddess later to be called Mary, she remained unmarried and had no regular consort. Hecate has survived in folklore as a 'hag' figure associated with witchcraft. Strmiska notes that Hecate, conflated with the figure of Diana, appears in late antiquity and in the early medieval period as part of an "emerging legend complex" associated with gatherings of women, the moon, and witchcraft that eventually became established "in the area of Northern Italy, southern Germany, and the western Balkans." This theory of the Roman origins of many European folk traditions related to Diana or Hecate was explicitly advanced at least, as early as 1807, as the Roman equivalent to the goddess Libertas. The Statue of Liberty is based on the Roman goddess Libertas, the Roman goddess of freedom. Originally, as goddess of personal freedom, she later became the goddess of the Roman commonwealth. Now she stands watch over The United States of America, the revived Roman Empire and spiritual Babylon.

The Queen of Babylon believed herself to be the incarnation of Lilith. We discussed Lilith in my first book, '*Creation Cries Out!*'.

Lilith was the origin of the vampire myths and

said to have been the serpent that deceived Adam and Even in the Garden. Semaramis who Ishtar in the She is the known as

So Lilith became became the Goddess religion of Babylon. fertility goddess EASTER!

Ishtar (Babylonian Semaramis) the fertility goddess of Easter is the Akkadian counterpart to the Sumerian Inanna and to the cognate northwest Semitic goddess `Ashtart. Anunit, Astarte and Atarsamain, the goddess of fertility and sexuality. The Babylonian fertility goddess Ishtar (Easter in English) is portrayed as a trinitarian god with Baal the Sun God/Tammuz the Sun of God/Ishtar the Queen of Heaven... this is where we get the Christian Trinity as incorporated into the "Christian Church" by the sun worshipping emperor Constantine at the Council of Nicaea.

The worship of the Babylonian Ishtar was survived and at the time of the Roman Empire was known as the Goddess of Liberty Libertas. This is the real spiritual implication behind The Statue of "Libertas".

In celebration of the centenary of the first Masonic Republic in 1884, the Statue of Liberty was presented to the Masons of

America, as a gift from the French Grand Orient Temple Masons. The Statue of Liberty is nothing more than a replica image of a pagan trinity goddess.

The Masonic "Torch of Enlightenment" was also referred to as the "Flaming Torch of Reason", by the Illuminati Masons in the

1700's and in 1884, the cornerstone for the Statue of Liberty was placed in a solemn ceremony, by the Masonic lodges of New York.

Below is the cornerstone of the Statue of Liberty dedicated to, and by, Freemasons. Below is the inscription dedicating the Statue of Liberty (Ishtar) by the Masonic Lodge who worships the founder of Masonry… Nimrod!

# ➤ Brigit –Irish Trinity

**Brigit – A "Christopagan" era Irish Trinity – The Celebration of Groundhog Day in the honor of the goddess Brigit and Catholic Nuns**

**Irish Catholic St. Brigit edallion.** The **goddess of the flame** to the ancient Celts, she has survived into <u>our time</u> as **"St. Bridget"** in the **Irish catholic church**. To this day her 'eternal flame' burns in Kildare, Ireland and her ancient sacred wells are still revered and visited. It is believed by pagan Catholics that Brigit, Lady of the Fairies – watches over their **sacred green** places and, if you look into her Magical Mirror, you can see the fairy realm. Here she is presented as a **cloverleaf Trinity**.

Brigit is known by various names, Brigit being the most ancient form. The name variations are: Brighid, Bride (Scottish), Brid, Brigit, Bridget, Brigantia (English), Brigan, Brigindo (Gaul) and Brigandu. Her name derives from her worship by the pre-christian Brigantes, who honored her as identical with Juno, Queen of Heaven.  Brigit was just another incarnation of Semaramis/Ishtar and the eternal flame. Into the 18th Century, her sacred flame was tended, at first, by priestesses, who later became catholic nuns, when **the pagan shrine became a convent**, at Kildare, Ireland. These nineteen virgin priestesses (called nuns by the Catholic Church) were called 'Daughters of the Flame'. No man was ever allowed near. In fact, these women had other women in the village bring them their necessary supplies so they wouldn't have to deal with men.  Bridget then became known as The Virgin Mary.

Imbolc **(Candlemas** and **Groundhog Day)**, the Celtic spring festival, honors Brigit. The Druids called this sacred holiday Oimelc, meaning "ewe's milk". Held on February 1st or 2nd, it celebrated the birthing and freshening of sheep and goats. The catholic version of Imbolc (Candlemas), also, involves much elaborate rituals and feasting, and to this very day, many Irish homes have a St. Brigit's cross for protection, still made from rushes as in days of old.

# ➤ Geryon Greek Trinity

### Geryon the 3 Headed God of Greek Mythology

In Greek mythology, Geryon (Ancient Greek: Γηρυών; gen.: Γηρυόνος), son of Chrysaor and Callirrhoe and grandson of Medusa, was a fearsome giant who dwelt on the island Erytheia of the mythic Hesperides in the far west of the Mediterranean. A more literal-minded later generation of Greeks associated the region with Tartessos in southern Iberia.

Geryon was often described as a monster with 3 human faces. According to Hesiod,X, Geryon had one body and three heads, whereas the tradition followed by Aeschylus gave him three bodies. As seen in the picture on the left, Geryon was a "Trinity" having 3 bodies, 3 heads, and 3 shields.

# ➤ Cerberus - Greek and Roman Trinity

### Trinity God Cerberus of Greek and Roman Mythology

Cerberus (pronounced /ˈsɜrbərəs/), or Kerberos, (Greek form: Κέρβερος, [ˈkerberos]) in Greek and Roman mythology, is a multi-headed hound (usually three-headed) which guards the gates of Hades, to prevent those who have crossed the river Styx from ever escaping. Cerberus is featured in many works of ancient Greek and Roman literature and in works of both ancient and modern art and architecture, although, the depiction and background surrounding Cerberus often differed across various works by different authors of the era. The most notable difference is the number of its heads: Most sources describe or depict three heads.

# The Hindu Trinity

### The Hindu Trinity

Idol worship and rituals are at the heart of Hinduism and have tremendous religious significance. All Hindu deities are themselves symbols of the abstract Absolute, and point to a particular aspect of the Brahman. The Hindu Trinity (Trimurti) is represented by three godheads: Brahma - the creator, Vishnu - the protector and Shiva - the destroyer.

The Hindu trinity is of Brahma, Vishnu and Shiva. They are respectively the creator, preserver and destroyer of the universe. They are also aligned as the transcendent Godhead, Shiva, the cosmic lord, Vishnu and the cosmic mind, Brahma. In this regard, they are called Sat-Tat-Aum, the Being, the Thatness or immanence and the Word or holy spirit. This is much like the Christian Trinity of God as the Father, Son and Holy Ghost. The trinity represents the divine in its threefold nature and function. Each aspect of the trinity contains and includes the others.

# ➤ The Viking Trinity

Trinity, Norway, 14 Century, CE

### The Viking Trinity

According to Adam of Bremen: "If plague and famine threatens, a libation is poured to the idol Thor; if war, to Odin; if marriages are to be celebrated, to Frey." Because Odin, the All-Father, was generally more feared than loved and subsequently kept at a distance, his son, Thor, assumed the position as favored deity. He was the protector and trusted friend. Some myths associated with Thor had him as almost human, with his foibles and gullibility.

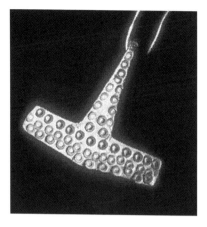

His hammer came to be used as an amulet, not only to signify the wearers allegiance to the old faith, but also as protection against the evils abounding. Later incorporated into Christianity and associated with The Cross of Tammuz.

Odin and Thor were the most prominent members of the militaristic Æsir family. Frey, god of fertility and fecundity, led the Vanir family, the early opponents of the Æsir. However, a truce between them brought Frey to Valhalla and elevated his status to be one of the Norse trinity. With the conversion to Christianity, the Norse trinity, although driven underground by the Christian church, nevertheless, remained significantly conspicuous, albeit in changed form.

# ➤ The Greek Trinity

**The Greek Trinity**

Olympic triad of Zeus (king of the gods), Athena (goddess of war and intellect) and Apollo (god of the sun, culture and music)

In the Greek culture, Zeus was the name for Nimrod, Athena for Semaramis, and Apollo for Tammuz.

47

# List of triple deities of Babylonian polytheism

## REFERENCE:
### HTTP://EN.WIKIPEDIA.ORG/WIKI/TRIPLE_DEITY#TRIPLE_GODDESSES

- The Classical Greek Olympic triad of Zeus (king of the gods), Athena (goddess of war and intellect) and Apollo (god of the sun, culture and music)
- The Delian chief triad of Leto (mother), Artemis (daughter) and Apollo (son)[35][36] and second Delian triad of Athena, Zeus and Hera·
- In ancient Egypt there were many triads, the most famous among them was that of Osiris (man), Isis (wife), and Horus (son), local triads like the Theban triad of Amun, Mut and Khonsu and the Memphite triad of Ptah, Sekhmet and Nefertem, the sungod Ra, whose form in the morning was Kheper, at noon Re-Horakhty and in the evening Atum, and many others.
- The Hellenistic Egypt triad of Isis, Alexandrian Serapis and Harpocrates (a Hellenized version of the previous), though in early Ptolomean religion Serapis, Isis and Apollo (who was sometimes identified with Horus)
- The Roman Capitoline Triad of Jupiter (father), Juno (wife), and Minerva (daughter).
- The Roman pleibian triad of Ceres, Liber Pater and Libera (or its Greek counterpart with Demeter, Dionysos and Kore)
- The Olympian demiurgic triad in platonic philosophy made up of Zeus (considered the Zeus [king of the gods] of the Heavens), Poseidon (Zeus of the seas) and Pluto/Hades (Zeus of the underworld), all considered in the end to be a monad and the same Zeus, and the Titanic demiurgic triad of Helios (sun when in the sky), Apollo (sun seen in our world) and Dionysus (god of mysteries, "sun" of the underworld) (see Phaed in Dionysus and the Titans)
- The Julian triads of the early Roman Principate:

- o Venus Genetrix, Divus Iulius, and Clementia Caesaris
- o Divus Iulius, Divi filius and Genius Augusti
- o Eastern variants of the Julian triad, e.g. in Asia Minor: Dea Roma, Divus Iulius and Genius Augusti (or Divi filius)
- The Matres (Deae Matres/Dea Matrona) in Roman mythology
- The Fates, Moirae or Furies in Greek and Roman mythology: Clotho or Nona the Spinner, Lachesis or Decima the Weaver, and Atropos or Morta the Cutter of the Threads of Life. One's Lifeline was Spun by Clotho, Woven into the tapestry of Life by Lachesis, and the thread Cut by Atropos.
- The Hooded Spirits or *Genii Cucullati* in Gallo-Roman times
- The main supranational triad of the ancient Lusitanian mythology and religion and Portuguese neo-pagans made up of the couple Arentia and Arentius, Quangeius and Trebaruna, followed by a minor Gallaecian-Lusitanian triad of Bandua (under many natures), Nabia and Reve female nature: Reva
- The sisters Uksáhkká, Juksáhkká and Sáhráhkká in Sámi mythology.
- The triad of Al-Lat, Al-Uzza, and Manat in the time of Mohammed (surah 53:19-22)
- Lugus (Esus, Toutatis and Taranis) in Celtic mythology
- Odin, Vili and Ve in Germanic mythology
- The Norns in Germanic mythology
- The Triglav in Slavic mythology
- Perkūnas (god of heaven), Patrimpas (god of earth) and Pikuolis (god of death) in Prussian mythology
- The Zorya or Auroras in Slavic mythology
- The Charites or Graces in Greek mythology
- The One, the Thought (or Intellect) and the Soul in Neoplatonism

# Summary of the pagan worship of The Trinity

The list of The Trinity as the fundamental description of "god" in pagan religions is quite long and really outside the scope of this book. My point here is to illustrate three very important truths:

1. There is no "Trinity" in the Bible, neither the word nor the concept.
2. The Trinity is a direct contradiction of The Shema, the mark of Yahuah.
3. The Trinity is the fundamental description of every pagan god.
4. Yahuah forbids us from saying we are worshipping Him yet doing so in the form of a pagan trinity.

I encourage everyone to research this topic on their own initiative. The names of Baal (Nimrod), Ishtar (Semaramis), and Tammuz

The "Entire" Earth is Lying in the Power of Ancient Babylon and the spell cast by Nimrod and his mother.

changed in each language but the religious practices did not. The main point I am making here with the concept of a pagan Trinity, is that the entire world and every religious system has been polluted by the worship of the Sungod Baal (Nimrod), Moon goddess Ishtar (Semaramis), and Tammuz their only begotten son (who was Baal in the flesh) in the form of a Trinity. The "Mystery" in the religion of Babylon was literally the "Mystery" of the Trinity. Satan is literally the "god of this world" and his counter to the ONE true God is his unholy Trinity. This "mark of the beast" has the minds of the entire Earth polluting every pagan religion, especially Christianity, the largest religion on Earth.

# Chapter 4

*Sunday worship of "Ba'al"*

# Sunday worship of Baal

*The Mystery Religion of Babylon* was the origin of Astrology, the worship of the planets in our solar system. Each planet was worshipped as a "god" and given a specific day of the week: Each of the days of the week, beginning on Sunday (the first day), is called a "Day of John". Each of the days of the week is called a "tentyon", a simple transcription of the Greek *ton theon* which means "the God". So each day of the week is named after The God represented by the stellar object. The hours and days are based not on Yahuah's Calendar found in the Bible, but pagan astrology and worship of the planets:

| Stellar Object → Day |
| :---: |
| **Sun → Sunday** |
| Moon → Monday |
| Mars → Tuesday |
| Mercury → Wednesday |
| Jupiter → Thursday |
| Venus → Friday |
| Saturn → Saturday |

http://en.wikipedia.org/wiki/Names_of_the_days_of_the_week

The pagan religions most "holy" worship day was the worship of the Sun on … Sunday. The reason why the Vatican has gone to a lot of trouble to convince everyone that our Messiah resurrected on "Sun-day" morning is because they want to assimilate him to the pagan god of the "Sun." Satan needed to find a way to convince the true followers of Messiah to worship him (Satan) unaware, and so he has set aside a special day that represents "Nimrod" the god of the sun from the Tower of Babel. Nimrod was the first historical false Messiah who ruled his false One World Government and

Religion about 2,275 years before the birth of the true Messiah Yahusha. He was the first historical Anti-Messiah whose name in Chaldean adds up to 666.

In order to "justify" the worship of Baal (the sungod) on Sunday, the Biblical reckoning of time where days started and ended at sunset, **was changed** to midnight. The Bible declares that the early church met "early on the first day of the week". This was actually referring to just 'after sunset' **on Saturday night** not Sunday morning. That would have been "late on the first day" in Jerusalem at the time it was recorded in The Bible. The early church was at home **keeping The Sabbath** with their families. Once the sun set on the Sabbath (7th day) (what we call Saturday night) they then met at a central place together that evening after the sun set which was "early the first day of the week". The first day (Sunday) was a work day for them and "early the first day" or late Saturday night after the Sabbath ended was the ONLY time they had to gather together. They had to go to work the next morning. Being a work day, no Jew was meeting together on what we call Sunday morning. It wasn't until Constantine changed The Sabbath to Sunday and gave everyone in his realm the day off that anyone could or would actually assemble on the first day.

Next, the pagan doctrine of Ishtar took hold and Good Friday/Easter Sunday was ordered by 'threat of death' to be observed instead of Passover and The Feast of First Fruits. I will cover this in detail in this book series.

Sunday worship is nowhere to be found in The Bible. This day is derived from "Sol," the Roman god of the sun. Their phrase for Sunday "Dies Solis" means "day of the sun." The Christian saint Jerome (d. 420) commented, attempting to justify Sunday worship, "If it is called the day of the sun by the pagans, we willingly accept this name, for on this day the Light of the world arose, on this day the Sun of Justice shone forth." None of that is commanded by Yahuah. Jerome just made it up and "justified" breaking what IS commanded, the 7th Day Sabbath, to keep himself from being killed in the inquisition. Again, all of this is covered in great detail in this book series. I mention it here with the intention to establish that "Sunday" was the Babylonian day of worship to the sungod *'The LORD'* (which means Ba'al) who is The Sungod.

The LORD is not the name of the Creator. The LORD is the name/title for the Babylonian sungod Ba'al and is a pagan reference to just about all pagan "gods"… The LORD is a false god:

> http://en.wikipedia.org/wiki/Baal
>
> **Baal**, *also rendered* **Ba'al** *(Biblical Hebrew בַּעַל), is a Northwest Semitic title and honorific meaning "master" or "lord" that is used for various gods who were patrons of cities in the Levant and Asia Minor, cognate to Akkadian Bēlu. A* **Baalist** *or* **Baalite** *means a worshipper of Baal i.e. The Lord.*
>
> *"Ba'al" or "The Lord" can refer to any god and even to human officials. In some texts it is used for Hadad, a god of the rain, thunder, fertility and agriculture, and the lord of heaven. Since only priests were allowed to utter His Divine name, Hadad, Ba'al was commonly used. Nevertheless, few if any Biblical uses of "Ba'al" refer to Hadad, the lord over the assembly of gods on the holy mount of heaven; most refer to a variety of local spirit-deities worshipped as cult images, each called ba'al and regarded in the Hebrew Bible in that context as a "false god".*
> *Etymology*
>
> **Ba'al** *(bet-ayin-lamedh) is a Semitic word signifying "The Lord, master, owner (male), keeper, husband",*

Yahuah told Elijah and Jeremiah that the Israelites would adopt "the way of the pagans" in Babylon who worshipped Ba'al and forget His name Yahuah; and that they would use the title *the LORD* which is a reference to Ba'al.

### 1 Kings 18

[18] "I have not made trouble for Israel," Elijah replied. "But you and your father's family have. <u>You have abandoned Yahuah's Commands and have followed Baal</u> (*The LORD*).

### Jeremiah 23

[25] "I have heard what the prophets say who prophesy lies in My Name. They say, 'I had a dream! I had a dream!' [26] How long will this continue in the hearts of these lying prophets, who prophesy the delusions of their own minds? [27] They think the dreams they tell one another will make My people forget My Name, <u>just as their ancestors forgot My Name through Baal</u> (*The LORD*) <u>worship</u>

The LORD "Ba'al" was worshipped on Sunday the "day of the invincible sun" or Dias Solis and the sacrifice to the LORD "Ba'al" was the pig of Ishtar (Easter). The prophecies in 1 Kings (that we would abandon Yahuah and follow Ba'al) have come true in Christianity, who calls on The LORD on Sunday putting their Faith in Easter (the sacrifice of a pig to Ba'al). Just as Jeremiah foretold, we would forget The Name Yahuah and use the LORD, as they did in Babylon.

We see below that The Name Yahuah was regularly pronounced by His chosen until superstitious Jews, who adopted the pagan practices of their captors, changed the name Yahuah to The LORD coming out of Babylonian captivity:

*The Encyclopedia Judaica*, Volume 7, pages 680-682

*Yahuah or Yahweh. The personal name of the God of Israel is written in the Hebrew Bible with the four consonants Yahuah and is referred to as the "Tetragrammaton". At least until the destructions of the First Temple in 586 b.c.e., <u>this name was regularly pronounced with its proper vowels (Yahuah)</u>, as is clear from the \*Lachish Letters, written shortly before that date. But at least by the third century*

> *b.c.e., the pronunciation of the name Yahuah was avoided,*
> *and Adonai, "the Lord", was substituted for it, as evidenced*
> *by the use of the Greek word Kyrios, "Lord", for Yahuah in*
> *the Septuagint, the translation of the Hebrew Scriptures*
> *that was begun by Greek-speaking Jews in that century.*
> *Where the combined form Adonai Yahuah occurs in the*
> *Bible, this was read as Adonai Elohim, "Lord God".*

We also see below, from the same source, that the Jews replaced the proper vowel points in Yahuah with the vowel points in Adonai giving us the name Yehowah in ERROR. Then uninspired Christian translators then came up with the totally foreign name Jehovah. In a total disconnect from all reality, the Jews started just saying ha-Shem (*the name*) and totally abandoned the proper Name of the Creator all together.

> *In the early Middle Ages, when the consonantal text of the*
> *Bible was supplied with vowels points to facilitate its*
> *correct traditional reading, the vowel points for 'Adonai*
> *with one variation - a sheva with the first yod of Yahuah*
> *instead of the hataf-patah under the aleph of 'Adonai were*
> *used for Yahuah, thus producing the form Yehowah. When*
> *Christian scholars of Europe first began to study Hebrew,*
> *they did not understand what this really meant, and they*
> *introduced the hybrid name "Jehovah". In order to avoid*
> *pronouncing even the sacred name Adonai for Yahuah, the*
> *custom was later introduced of saying simply in Hebrew*
> *ha-Shem (or Aramaic Shemc, "the Name") even in such an*
> *expression as "Blessed be he that cometh in the name of*
> *Yahuah" (Ps. 118:26).*

This is an abomination! It is literally "taking His name in vain". Vain means to bring to nothing by using titles!
Yahuah gave us His Name and He Declares that it is His Memorial for all generations:

## Exodus 3:15

And Yahuah said moreover unto Moses, Thus shalt thou say unto the children of Israel, Yahuah the God of your fathers, the God of Abraham, the God of Isaac, and the God of Jacob, hath sent me unto you: this is My Name forever, and this is My Memorial unto all generations.

His Name is not "The LORD" or "Adonai" or "Jehovah" or anything else. His name is YHVH (Yahuah in English) and that is His Everlasting memorial by which He is to be called upon. Our English Bibles use the title 'The LORD' for Yahuah which is a violation of the Command not to add to nor subtract from His Word. Not to mention, it is idolatry calling upon the Babylonian god Ba'al. We, humanity, have totally forgotten the name of our Creator which was originally written in His Word over 8,000 times! We replaced every reference to it with The LORD (Ba'al). Below we see the Jews committed this abomination out of what I call "reverent stupidity" as they followed the way of the pagans in Babylon:

### _Unger's Bible Dictionary_, on page 665:

_Lord (Hebrew, Adon), an early word denoting ownership; hence, absolute control. It is not properly a Divine title. The Jews, out of a superstitious reverence for the Name Yahuah, always, in reading, pronounce Adonai (lord) where YHVH is written._

### _Smith's Bible Dictionary_, 1872 Edition, states the following:

_The substitution of the word Lord is most (sad); for, while it in no way represents the meaning of the Sacred Name, the mind has constantly to guard against a confusion with its lower uses, and, above all, the direct personal hearing of the Name on the revelation of Yahuah...is injuriously out of sight._

This is extremely important as the name of the Messiah contains the Tetragrammaton to fulfill the prophetic requirements of the One name under heaven whereby we may obtain Salvation:

### Acts 4:12

Salvation is found in no one else, for there is *no other name* under heaven given to mankind by which we must be saved."

When I quote Scripture in this book, no matter what translation I use, I will always replace the pagan reference and title of The LORD with Yahuah and Lord with King as it applies to Yahusha. I will always clarify in context the use of impersonal pronouns such as 'he' and 'him' by identifying the subject by name. I will turn the text from passive voice to active voice. I will demonstrate when the uninspired translations are corrected in this way; the truth comes shining through as to the real meaning of the text. In doing so, many of the Scriptures used to justify the false doctrines of the incarnation and The Trinity completely fall apart in light of the Truth.

# Chapter 5
## *Christmas – "The Rebirth of The Sun"*

# The Birthday of Nimrod and Tammuz and the Rebirth of the Sun (Christmas)

The origin of Christmas has been and continues to be exposed for its true roots:

> *"Nimrod started the great organized worldly apostasy from God that has dominated this world until now. Nimrod married his own mother, whose name was Semaramis. After Nimrod's death, his so-called mother-wife, Semaramis, propagated the evil doctrine of the survival of Nimrod as a spirit being.*
>
> *She claimed a full-grown evergreen tree sprang overnight from a dead tree stump, which symbolized the springing forth unto new life of the dead Nimrod. On each anniversary of his birth, she claimed, Nimrod would visit the evergreen tree and leave gifts upon it. December 25th, was the birthday of Nimrod. This is the real origin of the Christmas tree."*
> **-The Plain Truth About Christmas by David J. Stewart**
>
> *"Traditionally, a yule log was burned in the fireplace on Christmas Eve and during the night as the log's embers died, there appeared in the room, as if by magic, a Christmas tree surrounded by gifts.*
>
> *The yule log represented the sun-god Nimrod and the Christmas tree represented himself resurrected as his own son Tammuz."*
>
> **--After Armageddon -Chapter 4 Where do we get our ideas? by John A. Sarkett**

The actual identity of "Santa Clause" is Nimrod himself and the X-mas Tree is a memorial to him.

We see Nimrod in a long white beard clearly pictured with a "Christmas Tree" and even a reindeer as early as 2000 BC, yes TWO THOUSAND YEARS before "Christianity" was ever created:

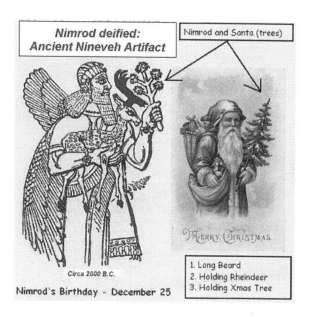

Nimrod deified: Ancient Nineveh Artifact

Nimrod and Santa (trees)

Circa 2000 B.C.

Nimrod's Birthday - December 25

1. Long Beard
2. Holding Rheindeer
3. Holding Xmas Tree

Christmas being the "birthday" of "Jesus" has its origins in the Babylonian Mystery Religion. In order to secure her reign as Queen of Babylon after Nimrod's death, Semaramis had to devise a way of keeping the "Spirit of Nimrod" alive. She had already deified Nimrod as Baal the Sungod but needed Nimrod to return to the people.

Semaramis consulted her astrologers who told her that the sun "dies" on December 21st (the shortest day of the year) but then it begins to come back to life again on the eve of December 24th as the days begin to grow longer.

> *"In paganism this is what is known as the "winter solstice," which falls on December 21st ----when the Earth is the furthest away from the sun. On December 24th, the Earth begins to rotate back around the sun and comes closer to the sun. But the pagans did not know this in earlier times before science and*

*telescopes. These pagans in Babylon thought that the sun died on December 21st and then it began to resurrect on the eve of December 24th and then it made its full rebirth on December 25th. They believed this to be the birthday of Nimrod or Baal the Sungod.*

*Using astrology as her guide, Semaramis became pregnant on around March 25th (9 months from December 25th), and then she concocted a legend for the Babylonian people telling them that on December 21st, Nimrod dies each year, but then on December 25th Nimrod is "born-again" as the "sun-god" or "Ba'al." Hence, on December 25th the "sun-god" is celebrated around the world with many different names.*

*Semaramis told the Babylonians that she had become the goddess of the moon and the sky and that Nimrod was being "reincarnated" in her womb as "Ba'al" the sun-god on December 25th. She told the Babylonians that Nimrod impregnated her with the "rays of the sun" supernaturally and Nimrod "re-incarnated" himself as her new son Tammuz on December 25th.*

*Her new son was named Tammuz according to Ezekiel 8:14 or generically he was called "Ba'al" (which means Lord or husband). Each year on Tammuz's birthday on December 25th, the pagans were ordered by Semaramis to go into the groves (forests) and placed a gift on a tree to honor Nimrod who was "cut down" like a tree. They were also ordered to cut down an evergreen tree, take it into their homes and decorate it with silver and gold balls to symbolize Nimrod's testicles.*

*Trees and branches became symbols of Nimrod because Nimrod was "cut down" by Shem, the son of Noah who placed a bounty hunt on his life. The book of Jasher tells us that it was Esau (the son of Jacob) who actually killed Nimrod. Hence, a tree stump became a place of honoring him, as the Scriptures speak of the pagans going into the "groves" or the forest and cutting down a tree, decorating it, and propping it up so that it will not totter."*

—

**...The Two Babylons, by Alexander Hyslop**

# How was "Christmas" passed down to us in "Christianity"?

In the pagan Roman society they instituted the "Saturnalia" in honor of the god Saturn. It was a Lawless celebration held on December 25th, the birthday of Tammuz and rebirth of Nimrod. Each year, an innocent person would be chosen by the communities as a human sacrifice to the gods. This person would be forced into engaging in all types of physical pleasures (food, sex, etc) throughout the week leading up to Saturnalia then murdered on December 25th with the aim of obtaining the gods blessing for the coming year's crops.

In addition to human sacrifice, there was wide-spread intoxication and the people would go house-to-house singing (origin of caroling). The people would mimic human sacrifice by eating human shaped biscuits (we call them **gingerbread men**). The Encyclopedia Britannica volume 24 page. 231 tells us the people would give each other gifts. Primarily to children in the form of "dolls" which represented sacrificed human beings to the infernal gods.

Christianity incorporated Saturnalia into the religion of Constantine (Christianity) calling it Christmas in the 4th Century AD. No such festival exists in the Bible. It is directly from Babylon. Yahusha was born during the Feast of Sukkoth in the Fall.

# The Christmas Tree

### Jeremiah 10:2-4

"Learn not the way of the heathen, and be not dismayed at
the signs of heaven; (astrology was idolized) for the
heathen are dismayed at them...For the customs of the
people are vain: for one cuts a tree out of the forest, the
work of the hands of the workman, with the axe. They deck
it with silver and with gold; they fasten it with nails and
with hammers that it move not." (then they put gifts under
it and bow down to it as if to accept the gift from the gods)

The Hebrew word for "groves" in this case is Strong's H842 –
'asherah אֲשֵׁרָה'.

*Asherah*: groves (for idol worship); *__a Babylonian__* (Astarte/Ishtar)
- Canaanite goddess (of fortune and happiness), the supposed
consort of Baal known as Ishtar, her images; the goddess,
goddesses; her images; sacred trees or poles set up near an altar.

The origin of the X-mas Tree (X or "the cross" is the symbol of
Tammuz and the mark/monogram of Jesus Christ) is actually the
Tammuz/Nimrod Tree and has absolutely nothing to do with The
Messiah or The Truth found in The Bible. The X-mas Tree was a
central figure in the Babylonian Religion with a snake wrapped
around a tree trunk. We now, of course, don't have snakes around
our tree, **we have garland**! But let us not be so naive to think
Yahuah approves of such ignorance in worship founded in
Babylonian paganism...

**It began with a Snake and a Tree**

Christmas trees are really Asherah poles or sacred trees for honoring "Ba'al" and the ornamental balls represent Nimrod's testicles! Garland represents the serpent, Satan! Babylonian history records that Nimrod was cut into pieces and his body parts were sent to different provinces of Babylon to warn the people not to sacrifice babies to Moloch. His only body part which was never

found was his penis. Semaramis, his mother/wife then decided to memorialize his penis by erecting a giant image of Nimrod's penis which today is called **the obelisk**. They adorn many Christian Churches today as steeples as I noted earlier in this chapter. We are COMMANDED by Yahuah to destroy these very structures: Exodus 23:24, Exodus 34:13, Deuteronomy 7:5, Deuteronomy 12:3, Jeremiah 43:13, Hosea 10:2. Yet, we openly worship them as part of the Christian Religion. The Christmas Tree is also the symbol of Satan in the Garden of Eden, the garland wrapped around the "Tree of Knowledge of Good and Evil" like a snake around the tree with the ornamental balls representing the forbidden fruit.

# Chapter 6
## The Cross... *"of Tammuz"*!

# The Cross of Tammuz

Tammuz, the second member of the pagan Babylonian Trinity, the incarnation of God in the flesh, is the false messiah of the religion

created by Semaramis (the Whore mentioned in Revelation). Yahuah has commanded us (His people) to "come out of her" and cease prostituting out the worship of the ONE true God to others.

The symbol of "the son of The LORD god Baal" in the pagan religion of Babylon was a cross. It is called *The*

*Cross of Tammuz.*

This cross was worn on the head dresses of the Babylonians and breastplates of priests and warriors alike in honor of Tammuz. The cross was a representation of "T" in Tammuz and his symbol "x".

The cross is a *tradition* of the Church, which our fathers have inherited, and is where we adopted the words "cross" and "crucify". These words are nowhere to be found in the Greek versions of the New Testament.

These words are mistranslations, a "later rendering", of the Greek words stauros and stauroo which mean stake and impale on a stake.

**Vine's Expository Dictionary of New Testament Words** says,

> "STAUROS denotes, primarily, an upright pole or stake ... Both the noun and the verb stauroo, to fasten to a stake or pole, **_are originally to be distinguished from_** the ecclesiastical form of a two-beamed cross. The shape of the latter had its origin in ancient Chaldea (Babylon), and was used as the symbol of the god Tammuz (being in the shape of the mystic Tau, **_the initial of his name_**) ... By the middle of the 3rd century A.D. at the Council of Nicea the churches had either departed from, or had travestied, certain doctrines of The Faith found in The Bible.

In order to increase the prestige of the apostate ecclesiastical system (known as Christianity) pagans were received into the churches **apart from regeneration by faith**, and were permitted largely to retain their pagan signs and symbols. Hence the Tau or T, in its most frequent form, with the cross piece lowered, was adopted and to this day remains the "symbol" of Jesus (Tammuz) or the X.

http://en.wikipedia.org/wiki/Christogram

> The most commonly encountered Christogram in English-speaking countries in modern times is the X (or more accurately, Greek letter chi) in the abbreviation Xmas (for "Christmas"), which represents the first letter of the word Christ.

We see that the "cross" is not in the Bible at all, but rather predates the New Testament in all pagan religions.

**Dr. Bullinger, in the Companion Bible, appx. 162, states,**

> "crosses were used as symbols of the Babylonian Sun-god (Tammuz)... Constantine was a Sun-god worshipper ... The evidence is complete, that Yahusha was put to death upon

*an upright stake, not on two pieces of timber"*

### Rev. Alexander Hislop, The Two Babylons, pp. 197-205,

*frankly calls the cross "this Pagan symbol ... the Tau, the sign of the cross, the indisputable sign of Tammuz, the false Messiah ... the mystic Tau of the Chaldeans (Babylonians) and Egyptians - the true original form of the letter T the initial of the name of Tammuz ... the Babylonian cross was* **the recognized emblem of __Tammuz__.***"*

### In the Encyclopaedia Britannica, 11th edition, vol. 14, p. 273,

*we read, "In the Egyptian churches the cross was a pagan symbol of life borrowed by the pagan-Christians and interpreted in the pagan manner." Jacob Grimm, in his Deutsche Mythologie, says that the Teutonic (Germanic) tribes had their idol Thor, symbolized by a hammer, while the Roman Pagans had their crux (cross). It was thus somewhat easier for the Teutons to accept the Roman Cross.*

Greek dictionaries, lexicons and other study books also declare the primary meaning of stauros to be an upright pale, pole or stake. The secondary meaning of "cross" is admitted by them to be a "later" rendering to accommodate Rome. At least two of them do not even mention "cross", and only render the meaning as "pole or stake".

In spite of this strong evidence and proof that the word stauros should have been translated "stake", and the verb stauroo to have been translated "impale", almost all the common modern versions of the Scriptures persist with the Latin Vulgate's crux (cross), a fallacious "later" rendering of the Greek stauros. Why then was the "cross" (crux) brought into the Faith? And why are our modern English Bibles implicit in this lie?

Again, historical evidence points to Constantine as the one who had the major share in uniting Sun-worship and the Messianic Faith into a modern day version of ***The Mystery Religion of Babylon***. We will look in depth at the history and evolution of Christianity in my next book, **Christianity:** *The Great Deception* and see exactly what happened.

Constantine's famous vision of "the cross superimposed on the sun", in the year 312, is usually cited. Writers, ignorant of the fact that the cross was not to be found in the New Testament Scriptures, put much emphasis on this vision as the onset of the so-called "conversion" of Constantine. But, unless Constantine had been misguided by the Gnostic Manichean half-Christians, who indeed used the cross in their hybrid religion, this vision of the cross superimposed on the sun could only be the same old cosmic religion, **the astrological religion of Babylon**. The fact remains: that which Constantine saw, is nowhere to be found in Scripture. But rather was a common symbol of his god… the Sungod. Constantine had just a few years prior converted to The Cult of Sol Invictus! Constantine worshipped Christos Mithras and the followers of Mithra were called Christians. I prove this too, in this book series. So looking up to his "sungod" seeing the cross of Tammuz should have been expected and understood for what it really was. There was a REASON why he was bowing down to the "sun" in the first place. Constantine did not convert to the Jewish High Priest and Messiah Yahusha. He converted the world to his existing religion that was known at that time as 'Christianity'.

We read in the book of Johannes Geffcken, The Last Days of Greco-Roman Paganism, p.319, "that even after 314 A.D. the coins of Constantine show an even-armed cross as a symbol for the Sun-god." This is the symbol of all sun worshipping religion as I have stated. This equidistant cross is the cut-out of the center of The Zodiac. Many scholars have doubted the "conversion" of Constantine because of the wicked deeds that he did afterwards, and because of the fact that he only requested to be baptized on his death-bed many years later, in the year 337. His coins to the day he died read "Sol Invictus Committi" or "committed to the invincible sun". The Catholic Encyclopedia even admits Constantine's conversion was a legend and should be stricken from our literature entirely.

### *Catholic Encyclopedia*, Farley ed., vol. xiv, pp. 370-1

> *The smooth generalization, which so many historians are content to repeat, that Constantine "embraced the Christian religion" and subsequently granted "official toleration", is "contrary to historical fact" and should be erased from our literature forever* (Catholic Encyclopedia, *Pecci ed., vol. iii, p. 299, passim).*

Simply put, Constantine was already a 'Christian' a follower of Christos Mithras and the Church acknowledges that the tale of his "conversion" and "baptism" are "entirely legendary". So, if the vision of the cross impressed him, and was used as a rallying symbol, it could not have been in honor of Yahusha, because Constantine continued paying homage to the Sun-deity and to one of the Sun-deity's symbols, **the cross** until the day he died. This continuation of Sun-worship by Constantine is demonstrated by the images of the Sun-deity on his coins that were issued by him up to the year 323. Secondly, the fact of his motivation to issue his Sunday-keeping edict in the year 321, which was not done in honor of Yahusha, but was done because of the "venerable day of the Invincible Sun". This edict is proof of Constantine's continued allegiance to Sol Invictus.

Where did the cross come from, then? J.C. Cooper, **An Illustrated Encyclopaedia of Traditional Symbols**, p. 45, aptly summarises it,

> *"Cross - A universal symbol from the most remote times; it is the cosmic symbol par excellence."* Yes, the cross is THE mark or cosmic symbol of The Zodiac of all pagan sun worshipping religions "par excellence". Other authorities also call it a sun-symbol, a Babylonian sun-symbol, an astrological Babylonian-Assyrian and heathen sun-symbol,

also in the form of an encircled cross referred to as a "solar wheel", and many other varieties of crosses. The cross with the sun in the background is taken directly from the center of The Zodiac:

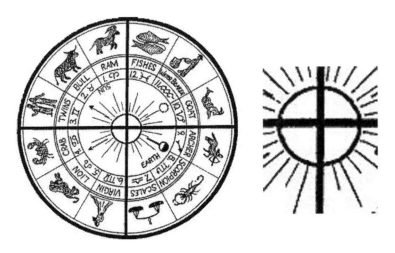

This symbol of the Sun from the center part of The Zodiac is the exact symbol of Christianity:

Also, "the cross represents the Tree of Life", the age-old fertility symbol, combining the vertical male and horizontal female principles, especially in Egypt, either as an ordinary cross, or better known in the form of the crux ansata, the Egyptian ankh (sometimes called the Tau cross), which had been carried over into our modern-day symbol of the female, well known in biology.

As stated above, the indisputable sign of Tammuz, the mystic Tau of the Babylonians and Egyptians, was brought into the Church chiefly because of Constantine, and has since been adored with all the homage due only to the Most High.

The Protestants have for many years refrained from undue adoration of, or homage to the cross, especially in England at the time of the Puritans in the 16th - 17th centuries. But lately this un-Scriptural symbol has been increasingly accepted in Protestantism and now widely believed to be a symbol of the Messiah.

We have previously discussed "the weeping for Tammuz", and the similarity between the Easter resurrection and the return or rising of Tammuz. Tammuz was the young incarnate Sun, the Sun-divinity incarnate. This same Sun-deity, known amongst the Babylonians as Tammuz, was identified with the Greek Adonis and with the Phoenician Adoni, and the Roman Mithras. All of them Sun-deities, being slain in winter, then being "wept for", and their return being celebrated by a festivity in spring, while some had it in summer - according to the myths of pagan idolatry.

The evidence for its pagan origin is so convincing that The Catholic Encyclopedia admits that "*the sign of the cross, represented in its simplest form by a crossing of two lines at right angles, greatly antedates, in both East and the West, the introduction of Christianity. It goes back to a very remote period of human civilization.*" That remote "period" they fail to identify is Babylon!

The Catholic Encyclopedia then continues reverence to the Tau cross of the pagan Egyptians, "*In later times the Egyptian*

*Christians (Copts), attracted by its form, and perhaps by its symbolism, adopted it as the emblem of the cross."* That is because the Egyptian god Horus was another incarnation of Tammuz. Further proof of its pagan origin is the recorded evidence of the Vestal Virgins of pagan Rome having the cross hanging on a necklace, and the Egyptians doing it too, as early as the 15th century B.C.E. The Buddhists, and numerous other sects of India, also used the sign of the cross as a mark on their follower's heads. The cross thus widely worshipped, or regarded as a 'sacred emblem', was the unequivocal symbol of Bacchus (Tammuz), the Babylonian Messiah, for he was represented with a head-band covered with crosses. It was also the symbol of Jupiter Foederis in Rome. Furthermore, we read of the cross on top of the temple of Serapis, the Sun-deity of Alexandria. This is Tammuz, whom the Greeks called Bacchus, with the crosses on his head-band.

After Constantine had the "vision of the cross", he and his army promoted another variety of the cross, the Chi-Rho or Labarum. The identical symbols were found as inscriptions on a rock, dating from the year ca. 2500 B.C., the time of Babylon the Great, being interpreted as "a combination of two Sun-symbols". The Ax or Hammer-symbol of the Sun- or Sky-deity is the ancient symbol of the Sun. These signs having a sensual or fertility meaning as well in the cult of Babylon.

Another proof of its pagan origin is the identical symbol found on a coin of Ptolemeus III from the year 247 - 222 B.C. A well-known encyclopedia describes the Labarum (Chi-Rho) as, "The labarum was also an emblem of the Chaldean (Babylonian) sky-god and in Christianity it was adopted..."Emperor Constantine adopted this Labarum as the imperial ensign and thereby succeeded in "uniting both divisions of his troops, pagans and Christians, in a common worship". According to Suicer, the word (labarum) came into use in the reign of Hadrian, and was probably adopted from one of the nations conquered by the Romans. "It must be remembered that Hadrian reigned in the years 76 - 138, that he was a pagan emperor, worshipped the Sun-deity Serapis when he visited Alexandria, and was vehemently anti-Judaistic, being responsible for the final near-destruction of Jerusalem in the year 130.

# The "Cross of Tammuz" and the Mark of the Beast

I go into great detail on this mark in my book, *The Antichrist Revealed!* I will cover some of that book here because this mark of the Cross of Tammuz, which represents the Babylonian Trinity, was the mark of that religion on their foreheads! This mark of Tammuz was depicted on the forehead of Aphrodite (Semaramis the mother of Tammuz). In the image above, we see the mark of the Cross of Tammuz on the forehead of the goddess Ishtar dating back to Babylon! What is the "mark of the beast" of which we read in Rev 13:16-17, Rev 14:9-11, Rev 15:2, Rev 16:2, Rev 19:20 and Rev 20:4 - a mark on people's foreheads and on their right hands? Rev 14:11 reveals the mark to be "the mark of his (the beast's) name." Have we not read about the mystic Tau, the T, the initial of Tammuz's name, his mark? This same letter T (Tau) was written in Egyptian

75

hieroglyphics and in the old Wemitic languages as, representing the cross.

This is the "mark" literally made on the foreheads of Christians in the Catholic Church. We are led as sheep to the slaughter into Babylonian worship of Tammuz in the image and name of "Jesus". This practice takes place in many protesting Catholic (Protestant) Churches across the world on "Ash" Wednesday! Following in the Babylonian tradition each year as they "mark" their followers with this same mark on their forehead:

 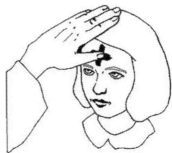

Let us rather use the true rendering of the Scriptural words stauros and stauro, namely "stake" and "impale" and eliminate the un-Scriptural "cross" and "crucify". The early Church Fathers attested to the use of the sign of the cross and that it is the Seal or Mark of Christianity; the mark that opposes The Shema.

Tertullian (d. ca. 250) described the commonness of the sign of the cross:

> *"In all our travels and movements, in all our coming in and going out, in putting on our shoes, at the bath, at the table, in lighting our candles, in lying down, in sitting down, whatever employment occupies us, **we mark our foreheads with <u>the sign</u> of the cross**" (De corona, 30).*

St. Cyril of Jerusalem (d. 386) in his Catechetical Lectures stated,

> *"Let us then not be ashamed to confess the Crucified. **Be the cross <u>our seal</u>**, made with boldness by our fingers on our brow and in everything; over the bread we eat and the cups we drink, in our comings and in our*

*goings out; before our sleep, when we lie down and when we awake; when we are traveling, and when we are at rest" (Catecheses, 13).*

Gradually, the sign of the cross was incorporated in different acts of the Mass, such as the three-fold signing of the forehead, lips, and heart. Ash Wednesday is the first day of Lent which is the Babylonian ritual of "Weeping for Tammuz". Occurring 46 days before Easter which is the sacrifice of a pig in honor of the death of Tammuz. At Masses and services of worship on Ash Wednesday, ashes are imposed on the foreheads of the "faithful".

# Chapter 7

## *The Resurrection of Tammuz… "Easter Sunday"!*

# The Resurrection Day of Tammuz (Easter)

Semaramis became known as the fertility goddess Ishtar. She took on many names in different cultures including Isis, Diana, Astarte, Ishtar, Aphrodite, Venus, and Easter. She was even identified with Mary as Mary was falsely deified and took on the titles "Mother of God" and "Queen of Heaven". Her son Tammuz took on many names as well such as Horus, Apollo, Sol, Krishna, Hercules, Mithra, and finally Jesus. The name Jesus H. Christ, in fact, originated by Constantine as Hesus Horus Krishna. "Hesus Horus Krishna" evolved into Jesus H. Christ over the years. All names of Tammuz put together for the son of the sungod and member of the Trinity worshipped on Sunday the day of his sungod. We will get to that in greater detail later in this book series.

Semaramis instituted a holy day in her Babylonian religion in honor of the supposed "death/resurrection" of her son Tammuz. Below is a picture of Semaramis and Tammuz, the "Madonna/Child" and "Mary/Jesus"…

Notice the "child" in these images is not a baby but a small fully developed man. While protesting Catholics (called Protestants) deny worship of this pagan deity… they indeed contradict that denial in action as they openly do just that on Sunday, Christmas and Easter.

In the previous images above we see to the left the idol of Ishtar/Tammuz renamed Jesus/Mary. In the middle we see the idol of the Madonna/Child renamed Jesus/Mary. We see a painting of Jesus/Mary on the right, all the exact same Babylonian deities. We need to begin admitting the obvious truth; these idols were not renamed because the pagans now believed in Yahusha the Messiah. No, Tammuz and Ishtar/Semaramis simply had their names changed in the false religion of Christianity which is a carbon copy of The Mystery Religion of Babylon! What we now call "halos" were nothing more than images of the Sun clearly demonstrating who these "paintings" were really representing. Not Yahusha but Tammuz. Not Miriam but Ishtar/Semaramis. The real truth behind the "cross of Jesus" and the "halos" around Jesus and Mary is simple. Jesus is Tammuz and Mary is Ishtar. They were the renamed and became the latest versions of the Babylonian Madonna and Child. This is clearly depicted below in the bottom right image as we see the images of the Sungod behind them with the X of Tammuz (the cross of the equinox from The Zodiac) over the sun behind Jesus' head. We see the crown on the Queen of Heaven and "Tammuz" in the upper right image of Jesus/Mary.

There still remains idols in the Vatican of "Tammuz the great hunter" to this day… their (Christianity's) REAL messiah they renamed Jesus or Hesus or Iesous or I.H.S. which means… Hail Zeus or Son of Zeus. The picture below is an idol of Tammuz "the Great Hunter" in the Vatican.

We pass on images of Tammuz (son of Semaramis) today as Cupid (the son of Venus). Still depicted as the "mighty hunter" complete with a bow and arrow!

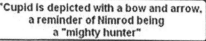

"Cupid is depicted with a bow and arrow, a reminder of Nimrod being a "mighty hunter"

Satan has very craftily hidden this Babylonian worship to target the minds of our children! We as adults have these "traditions" engrained in us and then we pass these abominations to Yahuah down to our children. The process continues generation after generation.

We were warned of this and it was prophesied to be true that, at this time in history, as Yahuah moves on His chosen in every nation:

### Jeremiah 16:19

Yahuah, my Strength and my Fortress, my Refuge in time of distress, to You the Gentiles will come out of the nations and will come back to You from the ends of the Earth and say, "Our ancestors possessed nothing but false gods, worthless idols that did them no good.

We need to wake up and realize every established religion, especially Christianity, has been polluted with The Mystery Religion of Babylonian gods, rituals, and worship. We still "hunt Ishtar eggs" in honor of Tammuz the Great Hunter on Ishtar's day and eat ham in his honor. We just call it by its English name Easter, but every ritual remains the same as in ancient Babylon.

No longer do we keep Passover and eat Lamb as commanded by The Messiah (strengthening The Law of Yahuah) as he kept Passover on the 14th of Abib (eve of Passover) just before he gave his body as The Passover Lamb. The last thing Yahusha said before dying on Passover was… ***KEEP PASSOVER!***

### Luke 22:19

19 And when he had taken some bread and given thanks (on the eve of Passover), He broke it and

gave it to them, saying, "This (Passover Dinner) is my body (*Passover Lamb*) which is given (*sacrificed*) for you; do this (*keep Passover*) in remembrance of me."

Do we obey our King? No… we now keep Ishtar and eat HAM because that is what was passed down to us from our ancestors. We literally eat the most abominable "beast" as defined in The Torah. We do this in honor of Tammuz who was killed by a pig. The fact that Jesus is in reality the Babylonian Tammuz, reincarnated Nimrod son of Ba'al, is denied by Christianity as **they have been given over by Yahuah to believe a lie**. I clearly define this "Spirit of Error" later in my book series. They have literally fallen for Nimrod / Semaramis / Tammuz under another name as they became Isis/Horus/Seb or **I.H.S** the monogram for Hesus Horus Krishna all names for Tammuz. Hesus Horus Krishna evolved into Jesus H. Christ in English. But in Latin it remains I.H.S. in the middle of Sol Invictus, the same "invincible Sun" worshipped from Nimrod to Constantine. This same pagan false messiah is worshipped world-wide today in Christianity!

IHS **is the very monogram of Jesus H. Christ** and is carried around by the High Priest of Ba'al to this day with the cross of Tammuz blazoned on top in the center of the Sun.

Proudly displaying to the world the truth on the back of his robe that he serves Ishtar, Horus, Seb as he places the symbol of sun worship on the heart of his goddess Ishtar (they simply changed her name to Mary).
This is pagan Babylonian sun worship as I will explain in detail in

my next book as we prove that the religion of Babylon was formally transferred to Rome and became what we know today as *"The Catholic Priesthood"*.

# Forty Days of Weeping for Tammuz: Lent & Ash Wednesday

When Tammuz was forty years old, hunting in the woods, he was killed by a wild boar (a pig). That is why we eat "ham" on Easter/Ishtar Day even though it is against Yahuah's Commandments to eat pork. Tammuz took after his father Nimrod in that he was a "mighty hunter." After Tammuz died, his mother Semaramis began a custom in Babylon called "forty days of weeping for Tammuz". People were commanded to fast and pray for Tammuz in the underworld. They exchanged one day of pleasure in this life for each year of Tammuz's life.

Today in the Roman Catholic Church this has been renamed "Lent." These forty days of fasting from something begins on what is called "Ash Wednesday" in the Catholic Church and many protestant Churches. The Cross of Tammuz is written "in ash" on the forehead of the "faithful". The priest takes ash and they draw a "mark" on our foreheads of a cross. The priest then recites a declaration "created from ashes and to ashes we shall return." We were all told that when we celebrate Lent, that we are commemorating the time when our Messiah fasted and prayed in the wilderness for "forty days and forty nights." This is a pagan lie. The truth of the matter is that our Messiah fasted and prayed during the "Forty Days of Repentance" leading up to Yom Kippur. It had NOTHING to do with "Lent" or Easter. Here we see Yahuah condemning this practice called "weeping for Tammuz" which today is called Lent:

### Ezekiel 8:13-14

"Turn you yet again, and you shall see greater abominations that they do. Then he brought me to the door of the gate of Yahuah's House which was toward the north; and, behold, there sat women <u>weeping for Tammuz</u>. Then said he unto me, Have you seen this, O son of man?"

Today, in many cultures, people make "Easter Bread" or "hot crossed buns". Do people realize that they are inadvertently offering up cakes to the Queen of Heaven?

### Jeremiah 7:18-19

"The children gather wood, and the fathers kindle the fire, and the women knead their dough, to make cakes to the queen of heaven, and to pour out drink offerings unto other gods, that they may provoke Me to anger. Do they provoke Me to anger? says Yahuah: do they not provoke themselves to the confusion of their own faces? Therefore thus says Yahuah your God; Behold, My anger and My fury shall be poured out upon this place."

No wonder the Catholic Church abolished the so-called Old Testament. It is a glaring condemnation of the entire religious system based in Rome.

Semaramis, (Nimrod's mother), became known in other cultures as "Magna Mater," the "Great Mother," and she was worshipped as Mother Earth. The Sun "mated" with the Earth each spring, and the "Rites of Spring" symbolized by the "May Pole" and "Easter" came 9 moons (months) before December 25th on the "birth" of the winter Sun. Her Assyrian name is Ishtar which is where we derive the name "Easter." Easter, the goddess of the dawn, is the universal goddess of fertility throughout history since the Tower of Babel. She began as Nimrod's wife Semaramis, and then after Yahuah scattered the nations and confused their languages at the Tower of Babel (Genesis 10-11), her image with her baby son Tammuz migrated to other nations under different names.

The Romans called her Astarte but later she was called Venus, and the Phoenicians called her Asherah. The Hebrews called her

Astoroth, the consort of Ba'al. Her emblem is the flower of the lily. She is the "goddess of the dawn," and her statue stands on a bridge in France. The French made a colossus of this image, and it now stands in New York Harbor, facing "East," referring to the name Ishtar or Easter. We call this idol of her **The Statue of Liberty.** Why is she facing East?

### Ezekiel 8:16

And he brought me into the inner court of Yahuah's House, and, behold, at the door of the Temple of Yahuah, between the porch and the Altar, were about five and twenty men, with their backs toward the Temple of Yahuah, and their faces toward the east; and they worshipped the sun toward the east.

The French Illuminati donated this statue to America in order to bring the spirit of Jezebel's influence upon our nation! I covered this earlier on the section on pagan Trinities. The torch that she carries is the "light of Lucifer" the same "light" of Freemasonry.

Easter is a day that is honored by nearly all of contemporary Christianity and is used to celebrate the resurrection of Jesus Christ which, now we know, is actually Tammuz, not Yahusha. This holiday often involves a church service at sunrise (sun worship), a feast which includes an "Easter Ham" (the abominable sacrifice), decorated eggs and stories about rabbits. Below is a quick summary of exactly "what" Easter is really all about.

# Detailed Origin of Easter

"Ishtar" (which is pronounced "Easter") was a day that commemorated the resurrection of one of their gods that they called "Tammuz". Tammuz was believed to be the only begotten son of the moon-goddess and the sun-god. In ancient times, there was a man named Nimrod, who was the grandson of one of Noah's son named Ham. Ham had a son named Cush who married a woman named Semaramis. Cush and Semaramis then had a son named "Nimrod."

After the death of his father, Nimrod married his own mother and became a powerful King. The Bible tells us of this man, Nimrod, in Genesis 10:8-10 as follows: "And Cush begat Nimrod: he began to be a mighty one in the Earth. He was a mighty hunter in the Face of Yahuah: wherefore it is said, even as Nimrod the mighty hunter in Face of Yahuah. And the beginning of his kingdom was Babel, and Erech, and Accad, and Calneh, in the land of Shinar." Nimrod became a god-man to the people and Semaramis, his wife and mother, became the powerful Queen of ancient Babylon.

Nimrod was eventually killed by an enemy, and his body was cut in pieces and sent to various parts of his kingdom. Semaramis had all of the parts gathered, except for one part that could not be found. That missing part was his reproductive organ. Semaramis claimed that Nimrod could not come back to life without it and told the people of Babylon that Nimrod had ascended to the sun and was now to be called "Baal", the sun god.

Queen Semaramis also proclaimed that Baal would be present on Earth in the form of a flame (representing the sun), whether candle or lamp, when used in worship. Semaramis was creating a mystery religion, and with the help of Satan, she set herself up as a goddess. Semaramis claimed that she was immaculately conceived.

She taught that the moon was a goddess that went through a 28 day cycle and ovulated when full. She further claimed that she came down from the moon in a giant moon egg that fell into the Euphrates River as she emerged as the moon fertility goddess Ishtar.

# The Easter Egg

This was to have happened at the time of the first full moon after the spring equinox. Semaramis became known as "Ishtar" which is pronounced "Easter", and her moon egg became known as the "Ishtar's" egg."

Every year, on the first Sunday after the first full moon after the spring equinox, a celebration was made. It was Ishtar's Sunday and was celebrated with rabbits and eggs. The "Ishtar Eggs" were dyed in the blood of babies sacrificed to Tammuz with the "cross of Tammuz" emblazoned on them as the children would "hunt" the eggs in the likeness of Tammuz and Nimrod the mighty hunters.

Ishtar also proclaimed that because Tammuz was killed by a pig, that a pig must be eaten on Ishtar's Sunday. At this point we begin to "see" what exact abominable "beast" replaced the sacrifice of the Passover Lamb. It was then and is still, the Easter Pig of Ishtar! I will go into this in detail later in this book series.

88

# The Easter Bunny

Tammuz was noted to be especially fond of rabbits, and they became sacred in the ancient religion, because Tammuz was believed to be the son of the sun-god, Baal. The rabbit is one of the most fertile creatures on Earth and held sacred to the fertility religion that Semaramis had created in Babylon. Ishtar was the fertility goddess and the Ishtar/Easter Rabbit was her symbol.

Easter egg hunting originated with Tammuz, like his supposed father, became a hunter. The day came when Tammuz was killed by a wild pig. Queen Ishtar told the people that Tammuz was now ascended to his father, Baal, and that the two of them would be with the worshippers in the sacred candle or lamp flame as Father, Son and Spirit.

# The Evergreen Tree and Lent and Fasting

Ishtar, who was now worshipped as the "Mother of God and Queen of Heaven", continued to build her mystery religion. The queen told the worshippers that when Tammuz was killed by the wild pig, some of his blood fell on the stump of an evergreen tree, and the stump grew into a full new tree overnight. This made the evergreen tree sacred by the blood of Tammuz. She also proclaimed a forty day period of time of sorrow each year prior to the anniversary of the death of Tammuz. During this time, no meat was to be eaten. We know this today as Lent.

# The Cross of Tammuz

Worshippers were to meditate upon the sacred mysteries of Baal and Tammuz, and to make the sign of the "T" in front of their hearts as they worshipped. Today this is called "The Sign of the Cross" made over the hearts of Christians as we read from the Catholic Encyclopedia:

http://www.newadvent.org/cathen/13785a.htm

*The cross was originally traced by Christians with the thumb or finger on their own foreheads. This practice is attested by numberless allusions in Patristic literature, and it was clearly associated in idea with certain references in Scripture, notably Ezekiel 9:4 (of the mark of the letter Tau); Exodus 17:9-14; and especially Apocalypse 7:3, 9:4 and 14:1. Hardly less early in date is the custom of marking a cross on objects — already Tertullian speaks of the Christian woman "signing" her bed (cum lectulum tuum signas, "Ad uxor.", ii, 5) before retiring to rest—and we soon hear also of the sign of the cross being traced on the lips (Jerome, "Epitaph. Paulæ") and on the heart (Prudentius, "Cathem.", vi, 129).*

# Hotcross buns

They also ate sacred cakes with the marking of a "T" or cross on the top. We know them today as "hotcross buns" we bake and eat them on "Ishtar Sungod Day" i.e. Easter Sunday.

# Chapter 8

## *Good Friday Sacrifice of Tammuz and "Venus Worship"*

# Good Friday - Venus Worship

Semaramis, (the wife and mother of Nimrod) who was also called Venus in Rome, has a day of the week named after her. That day in Italian or Latin is "Venerdi" for Venus. This word "Venerdi" is where we get the word "venerate" which means "to worship." In the 3rd Century, Constantine named the statue of Venus "The Virgin Mary." As I demonstrated before, the days of our "week" are pagan in origin as they worshipped the heavenly bodies:

| Stellar Object → Day |
| --- |
| Saturn → Saturday |
| **Sun → Sunday** |
| Moon → Monday |
| Mars → Tuesday |
| Mercury → Wednesday |
| Jupiter → Thursday |
| Venus → Friday |

Hence "Friday" is meant to signify her participation with the crucifixion of the Messiah! The Roman Catholic Church states in their Catechism that Mary is the "co-mediator, co-redeemer, & mediatrix" with the Messiah! And of course this is utter blasphemy and completely unscriptural! They teach that she participated in the crucifixion and that she is the co-redeemer with our Messiah! Now certainly, we can see that as his mother, she would've suffered and she was grief stricken over watching her son be tortured to death. But never-the-less, the idea of calling her a "co-mediator" is idolatry, and blasphemy. This treats her as a "goddess" worthy of worship instead of the mortal human being that she was. The Catholic Church has now deified Mary and proclaimed her "Mother of God" and "Queen of Heaven" all titles of Semaramis.

# Chapter 9
## *Name Changes throughout Cultures*

# Name changes throughout language and culture

# NIMROD

The violent death of Nimrod can be seen in the death of Osiris, which is the central focus of all pagan religions of ancient Egypt.

1. EGYPT= Osiris

2. Greece= Bacchus- God of wine- refiner of souls.

3. The horned One= Kronos-Saturn

4 The Man - Bull in Assyria

5. The winged Bull =Babylon Marduk- In the decor of the halls of Berlin.

6. The Centaur = half horse - half man Greek Mythology

7. Bel - Belus - Satan comes in many ways to deceive

8. Krishna in India

9. Jupiter and Zeus in Rome.

# TAMMUZ

In death, she would have him worshipped as "The Woman's Seed" (Zero-Ashta): The seed of Ashta or Ashtoreth who was destined to bruise the serpents head and in so doing had his own heel bruised.

The death of Nimrod brings the resurrected Tammuz as child in his mother's arms. Semaramis (Nimrod's wife) is made a goddess and worshipped as Madonna and child. Later as Mary became the mother of Jesus, carrying Jesus, which started in Ephesus. They worshipped Tammuz as resurrected King.

Tammuz throughout cultures:

1. Horus – Egypt

2. Mithra - Persian

3. Krishna - Eastern

4. Thor - Viking

5. Apollo – Greek

6. Hesus – Druids

7. Jesus - Modern

# SEMARAMIS

At the death of Nimrod, his wife Semaramis was elevated to goddess and as co-builder of Babylon. She was also the wife of Nimrod and wife/mother of Tammuz.

Semaramis took the image of the "Mother of Nimrod" rather than his wife. Mother and son worship was then renamed Jesus and Mary and the abomination was complete. Little child in mother's arms became the image of the god of confusion.

NAMES OF SEMARAMIS (THE ORIGINAL JEZEBEL SPIRIT)

1. Queen of Heaven
2. Virgin Mother
3. Beltis- female of Baal
4. Madonna and child- Council of Ephesus condoned the worship of Mary and the spirit of the harlotry came into the church doctrine in 431 A.D.
5. Athena in Greece birthed out of the head of Zeus. (Jupiter Acts 19). Apis Bull cult golden calf at the foot of Mt. Sinai (obedience).
6. Cybil
7. Rhea
8. Ashtoreth in Palestine ( 1Sam. 7:3).
9. Ishtar (Easter) decorates the gate of Babylon
10. Diana of the Ephesians
11. Venus (goddess of love)
12. Artemis
13. Astarte
14. Holy Mother
15. Isi and son Iswara
16. She shares with Nimrod the goddess of fortifications (strongholds).

# Conclusion
## *The Mystery Religion of Babylon*

# Summary of the Mystery Religion of Babylon

We are Commanded both by The Creator and His Messiah to come out of this abomination called Mystery Babylon and not to Worship our Creator the way the pagans worship their gods. It is an abomination to Yahuah:

### Deuteronomy 12:4

...3"You shall tear down their altars and smash their sacred pillars and burn their Asherim with fire, and you shall cut down the engraved images of their gods and obliterate their name from that place. 4" You must not Worship Yahuah your God in their way.. 5"But you shall seek Yahuah at the place which Yahuah your God will choose from all your tribes, to establish His Name there for His dwelling, and there you shall come....

### Revelation 17:5

The name written on her forehead was a mystery: Babylon the great the mother of prostitutes and of the abominations of the Earth.

### Revelation 18:4

3"For all the nations have drunk of the wine of the passion of her immorality, and the kings of the Earth have committed acts of immorality with her, and the merchants of the Earth have become rich by the wealth of her sensuality." 4I heard another voice from heaven, saying, "Come out of her, My people, so that you will not participate in her sins and receive of her plagues; 5for her sins have piled up as high as heaven, and Yahuah has remembered her iniquities....

I want to encourage us all to inspect our lives, what we believe, how we worship. This has been a very long detailed exposition of the religion born in Babylon. One that must be understood as we identify the "Great Deception" that, if possible, could even deceive the very chosen sons of Yahuah. This deception is identified as The Mystery Religion of Babylon.

**Matthew 24:24**

For false messiahs and false prophets will appear and perform great signs and wonders to deceive, if possible, even the elect.

Let me clearly and simply summarize what this religion is:

- The Worship of The Trinity in any form
- The worship of the Sun on dies Solis the "day of the sun" or Sunday
- The worship of the death/resurrection of Tammuz on Ishtar (Easter) Sungod Day
- The adoration of the Madonna and Child
- The adoration of the Cross of Tammuz
- The 40 days of Weeping for Tammuz
- The celebration of Christmas the birthday of the sun/Baal/Tammuz
- The celebration of Valentine's Day (Cupid is Tammuz)
- The worship of Hesus Horus Krishna all names of Tammuz shortened to Jesus H. Christ in place of Yahuah the ONE and ONLY God.

**John 17:3**

Now this is Eternal life: that they know you Yahuah, **the Only True God**, and (come to you through) The Messiah Yahusha, whom you have sent (as a substitute for sin).

99

### 1 Corinthians 8:6

Yet for us there is but One God, the Father Yahuah, from Whom all things exist and for Whom we live; and there is but one King, Yahusha the Messiah, for whom all things were created (as an inheritance by Yahuah for Yahusha) and through whom we have Eternal life (in covenant).

- The worship of a man above Yahuah as God and the belief in any form of an incarnated God-man.

In short, the Mystery Religion of Babylon is any Sunday / Christmas / Easter / Jesus / Trinity church complete with an obelisk (steeple) and the cross of Tammuz on top. That today is the modern day Mystery Religion of Babylon compliments of the Roman Emperor Constantine who was a sun worshipper until his death. The very Constantine who believed himself to be the incarnated Apollo (Tammuz) in the flesh. No wonder he was kneeling down toward the EAST worshipping the Sun and saw a "cross"! He was worshipping Baal and saw the sign of Tammuz just like we should have expected him to.

He did not convert to a follower of the Hebrew Messiah Yahusha and a servant of Yahuah. In fact, he went on to wage an all-out war against the Truth and The Faith. He converted the world to his religion by the threat of death (the inquisition) and then burned all the documents that would incriminate him. Ownership of books of any kind were banned this is known as The Dark Ages to "seal" this abomination so that it would never be questioned. He then changed the Ordained Feasts of Yahuah, changed His Sabbaths, abolished His Laws, and changed the name of the Messiah to "Heil Zeus" Hesus Horus Krishna (Jesus H. Christ).

No longer did the Messiah's name call out to and give Glory to Yahuah as does the name Yahusha (means Yahuah's Salvation) but now it gave glory to Constantine's god, Zeus, in the literal name of the son of Zeus/Nimrod… TAMMUZ. Every pagan festival remained the same down to the very last detail. This "new" religion was not in fact "new" **but the ancient Babylonian Religion** and he called his new (revamped) universal religion of Babylon... "Christianity"! It's seat... **Rome**. Where it remains today.

In my next book, '*Christianity and The Great Deception'*, we will take a detailed look into "how" this happened. We will dig deep into church and historical records. We will trace this abomination as all religion were merged into one known as syncretism. It was through Hellenism that the largest religion on Earth, Christianity, was born by merging all religions together. That is why it is the largest religion on Earth. It is the 'wide gate' that incorporates all religions into one universal religion that leads to destruction:

# **Matthew 7:13**

¹³ "Enter through the narrow gate; for the gate is wide and the way is broad that leads to destruction, and there are many who enter through it. ¹⁴ For the gate is small and the way is narrow that leads to life, **and there are few who find it**.

If you are one of the chosen few, then continue with me on this journey in my book series, The Original Revelation Series, as we continue to peel back the layers of pagan influence to find The Way, The Truth, and The Life. We are on our search for the true Faith, the original revelation given to mankind and passed down through Abraham, Isaac, Jacob, Moses, Yahusha, and then to the early church.

## BOOK 1: CREATION CRIES OUT!

In this book I trace the great deception back to its origin and explain how the "Gospel message in the stars" was corrupted into another gospel. I re-establish the message contained in the Heavenly Scroll and give Yahuah the Glory He deserves as the Creator of all things. In this book, the original revelation found written in the stars is broken down, defined, and glorified. I explain how the watchers corrupted the true message and taught mankind to worship the creation over the Creator. Creation Cries Out! Reveals the secrets preserved in the Heavens, and provides clear instruction so that the Great Seal over the Bible and the books of prophecy can be opened. Every prophet of Yahuah based their predictions on the Heavenly Scroll and described it in great detail.

## BOOK 2: MYSTERY BABYLON THE RELIGION OF THE BEAST

In this book I explain how that corrupted message was formulated into a formal religion in Babylon and define that religion as it existed then. We will go back to the very beginning of "paganism" and examine the gods and rituals that define this false religion. We will trace this religion, show how it evolved, who created it, and how it came to dominate all mankind. This information is vital as there is prophesied to be, at the end, a religion on Earth based on Mystery Babylon that deceives all humanity. The only way to properly identify that religion today that has fulfilled this prophecy is to fully understand Mystery Babylon.

## BOOK 3: 'CHRISTIANITY AND THE GREAT DECEPTION'

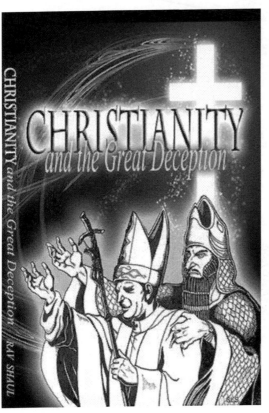

I compare Christianity to Mystery Babylon and prove that it is a carbon copy and is the prophesied false religion. Every description of "God" is taken directly from Babylon. From the Trinity to calling the Creator "The LORD" are all based on sun worship. I explain where Jesus H. Christ came from, who created that false image, and how that false messiah is a carbon copy of the second member of the Babylonian Trinity named Tammuz. From the false sacrifice of a pig on Easter, to Sunday worship, to Christmas… every aspect of the Christian Religion is a carbon copy of Mystery Babylon! I document everything carefully from historical sources, the Catholic Church documents, and the Bible. No one who has read this book has remained a "Christian" after finishing it.

## BOOK 4: 'THE ANTICHRIST REVEALED!'

In this book I prove that Jesus H. Christ is the false image of the true messiah, and I demonstrate how he meets every prophecy of the "Antichrist". I define in great detail such things as the Abomination of Desolation, the Spirit of the Antichrist, the Spirit of Error, the other Gospel, and much more. In this book, I demonstrate through Biblical prophecy that the false messiah is an "image" of the true Messiah not an actual person. This book is 500 pages of solid proof that the "god" of this Earth, Jesus Christ is the "Abominable Beast" foretold by name, sacrifice, and rituals. I prove that "Jesus" is not the name of the Messiah in any language much less Hebrew. We dissect that name and prove how the name of the Messiah was intentionally altered to give glory to Zeus over Yahuah. The true name of the Messiah is Yahusha.

## BOOK 5: 'THE KINGDOM'

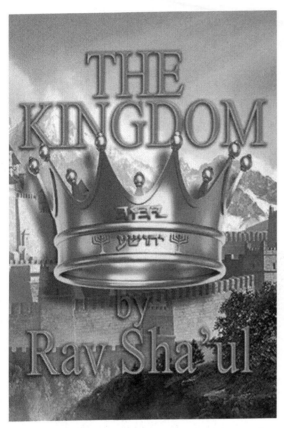

With the false religion, the false messiah, the false sacrifice, the false rituals clearly defined in the first 4 books, I begin to relay a firm foundation in what is true. In this book I define The Kingdom of Yahuah in great detail. I explain how all previous 6 covenants were transposed into the final 7th Covenant of Yahusha. I breakdown every aspect of the Kingdom using physical to spiritual parallels of a kingdom on Earth. What is this Kingdom, what is its purpose, what is its domain, who is its King, what is its constitution, who are its citizens, and what responsibility to the citizens who gain citizenship? All answered in this book.

# BOOK 6: 'THE YAHUSHAIC COVENANT VOLUME 1 - THE MEDIATOR'

In this book I break down The New Covenant and explain who Yahusha is in relation to Yahuah, what our roles are in the covenant of Yahusha, and much more. The Yahushaic Covenant is the "Salvation of Yahuah Covenant". I explain the role the Law plays in our lives under covenant with Yahusha. I explain the effects of Hellenism and blending the truth with paganism. I breakdown the scripture in context, shedding light on the writings in the Renewed Covenant with the original scriptures (Old Testament if you must). I re-teach the scriptures in light of the ancient language and cultural matrix of the 1st Century people of Yahuah living in the land of Israel.

## BOOK 7: 'THE YAHUSHAIC COVENANT VOLUME 2 - THE LAW AND THE SHA'ULINE DOCTRINE'

In this book, I explain the role the Law plays in our lives and re-teach Sha'ul's writings from the standpoint of intent. I overcome the Christian lie that Sha'ul taught against the Torah. We go in and take a hard look at how Sha'ul's writing were translated and "twisted" by the Greeks into another Gospel called The Pauline Doctrine. In this book, I introduce us all to Rav Sha'ul the leader of the Nazarenes! What does that mean, and what does that one fact say about the way his writings have been translated today? I explain the various aspects of The Law, how it was transposed over time from the Mind of Yahuah, to written in the stars at creation, to given orally, to written in stone, to finally written on our hearts. I explain the various jurisdictional aspects of the Law, look at the Law from the standpoint of intent, and provide solid instruction to the Nazarene today in how to approach the Law of Yahuah.

## BOOK 8: 'THE YAHUSHAIC COVENANT VOLUME 3 - MELCHIZEDEK AND THE PASSOVER LAMB'

What does Melchizedek really mean? In this book I explain how Yahusha became the King of Kings and the Eternal High Priest by blood lineage to King David and the ordained Zadok Priesthood. We travel back 2,000 years to the time of the Messiah's birth to fully understand the mindset of that time. A time of great expectation toward the coming Messiah. We look back into historical documents surrounding that time period to identify the lineage of Yahusha. Lineage that was lost to antiquity when Rome burned the original manuscripts. Who were Yahusha's "other grandparents" that contributed equally to his bloodline, we have just never been introduce to? How is Yahusha "King of Israel". How is Yahusha the "High Priest of Israel". The Bible declares Yahusha inherited those titles. If so, how and from whom? This book is a must read and introduction to the REAL Messiah in a way you have never known him.

## BOOK 9: 'THE NARROW GATE'

In this book I explain how keeping the Feasts of Yahuah properly is a pre-requisite of entering the Kingdom. The Feast Cycle is the "Narrow Gate" of a wedding and we must rehearse these events from the standpoint of "a Bride". What is the true meaning of the feasts, what are they rehearsing, how do we keep them? All these questions are answered and more in the final book in this series, The Narrow Gate.

## BOOK 10: THE MISTRANSLATED BOOK OF GALATIANS

The letter to the Galatians is one of the most mistranslated (purposely) books in the Bible. The Greeks twisted the words of Sha'ul into a lie to abolish the Law.

In this book, I go verse by verse showing were and how the words were twisted, showing the proper translation, and then using all of Sha'ul's writing to shed light on what Sha'ul was talking about in this letter. The resulting translation is the first of its kind! The real letter to the Galatians says the exact opposite of what you read in your English Bibles. The basic foundation of the Christian Church is found to be a lie and the truth revealed in this book about what Sha'ul actually taught concerning The Law, Circumcision, and many other things.

## BOOK 11: THE NAZARENE

The true Messiah was a Nazarene. What does that mean exactly? Who were The Nazarenes, what did they believe, and what happened to them? What does it mean to be a Nazarene today? This book will change the way you see Yahusha the Nazarene. I go into depth about who Yahusha was defining his humanity vs his divinity. This book is an all out assault on the Spirit of the False Messiah! Each page will have you putting the book down to just say "Wow!". I explain how Yahusha serves as Eternal High Priest and by what authority. How Yahusha is the King of Kings and what they means. The Nazarene is 600 pages of truth and history hidden from us all for 2,000 years by tradition and religion and a "must have"! It will change your life.

All Glory belongs to Yahuah. He is our Creator, Author of the Heavenly Scroll, and Father of the called out ones (Nazarenes). And to Yahusha the Nazarene, the Messiah and Royal High Priest of Israel, I say...

"WORTHY IS THE LAMB! TO RECEIVE HONOR, AND GLORY, AND POWER, AND PRAISE"

HALLELUYAHUAH

LET IS BE SO DONE, ON EARTH AS IT IS WRITTEN IN THE HEAVENLY SCROLL.

Kingdom blessings, and much love…

Rav Sha'ul

*If this book has been a blessing to you, please support this ministry.  Click on the donate button at www.sabbathcovenant.com*